THE
5 MINUTE
RESET

SIMPLE MINDFULNESS
TECHNIQUES FOR A BUSY LIFE

ADAM C NORTON

Contents

Contents

Chapter One

Introduction

Why Mindfulness Matters

Life moves fast, and so do we. With endless responsibilities, notifications, and distractions, it can feel impossible to pause and catch your breath. Yet, the very moments when life feels the most overwhelming are when we most need to stop, reset, and reconnect.

If you've ever felt stuck in a cycle of stress, overthinking, or exhaustion, you're not alone. Most of us try to power through, telling ourselves we'll rest once we've crossed the next item off our to do list. But what if the secret to finding calm and focus isn't about doing more—it's about doing less?

This is where mindfulness comes in. Mindfulness isn't about silencing your thoughts or escaping life's demands. It's about showing up—fully present, fully aware—in your own life. It's about recognizing when you're on autopilot and choosing, instead, to engage with the moment in front of you.

In a world that glorifies busyness, mindfulness is a quiet rebellion. It's a reminder that rest isn't a reward for productivity—it's a necessity for living well.

What This Book Offers

This book is your guide to reclaiming calm, focus, and balance through small, intentional resets. You'll learn simple, practical techniques that fit seamlessly into even the busiest schedules. Whether you have five minutes or just one, these tools will help you find clarity and connection in the midst of life's chaos.

Each chapter introduces a new tool for your mindfulness toolkit:

- Breathing exercises to calm your mind and body.

- Journaling techniques to process thoughts and emotions.

- Grounding practices to center yourself during stressful moments.

- Gratitude journaling to shift your mindset toward positivity.

- Affirmations and visualizations to reframe your inner dialogue.

- Mindful movement and nature connection to energize and reset.

By the end of this book, you'll have a personalized system of practices that empower you to pause, reset, and show up with greater presence and intention.

Why 5 Minutes?

You might be wondering: can something as small as a 5-minute reset really make a difference? The answer is yes. Small moments of mindfulness have a cumulative impact. They're like drops of water filling a glass—over time, these small pauses build resilience, clarity, and balance.

Think of a 5-minute reset as a mental pit stop. It's not about solving every problem or achieving perfect calm—it's about giving yourself the space to breathe, reflect, and recharge.

Who This Book is For

Whether you're new to mindfulness or looking to deepen your practice, this book offers accessible tools for anyone who feels overwhelmed, distracted, or disconnected. It's for parents juggling endless tasks, professionals navigating deadlines, students managing stress, or anyone craving a moment of calm in a noisy world.

The goal isn't perfection. It's progress. By starting small and staying consistent, you'll discover that mindfulness isn't a destination—it's a way of moving through life.

Your Journey Starts Now: Your journey to calm, clarity, and balance starts with understanding the power of a 5-minute reset. In the next chapter, we'll explore how these brief, intentional pauses can transform your mindset, energize your day, and create space for meaningful change.

Chapter Two

The Magic of a 5-Minute Mindset

Let's face it—life moves fast. Some days, it feels like there aren't enough hours to get everything done, let alone carve out time for yourself. If you're like most people, your to-do list probably resembles an epic novel, and no matter how much you cross off, there's always something waiting to be added. Between work, family, social commitments, and the elusive "me time," it's no wonder many of us feel like we're constantly on the edge of burnout.

But here's a secret: finding balance doesn't require hours of meditation or a week-long retreat in a cabin. Sometimes, all it takes is five minutes—a tiny slice of your day dedicated to resetting your mind and regaining control. Think of it as a mental pit stop, a moment to refuel before you dive back into life's chaos.

Imagine this: you're overwhelmed, juggling deadlines and distractions, and everything feels like it's spinning out of control. Instead of letting stress snowball, you pause. You take a deep breath, let your shoulders relax, and close your eyes for a moment of stillness. That's the essence of a five-minute mindset—a deliberate choice to stop, recalibrate, and approach life with renewed clarity.

Why does this work? Because it interrupts the cycle of stress and gives your brain a chance to reset. Think of it like rebooting a computer that's frozen. Those brief moments of mindfulness help clear out the mental clutter and create space for calm and focus. You're not just reacting to life's chaos; you're taking charge of how you respond.

And the best part? You don't need fancy tools, special training, or hours of free time to make it happen. A five-minute mindset shift is portable. It can happen anywhere—while you're at your desk, waiting in line, or even sitting in your car before heading into the next task on your list. It's simple, effective, and completely within your control.

These five-minute resets are more than just stress relief—they're an opportunity to build resilience. Over time, these moments of calm can become the foundation for a more balanced, mindful life. They remind you that even in the busiest days, you have the power to pause, breathe, and reset.

Let this chapter be your invitation to embrace those five minutes, not as a luxury, but as a necessity. Because when you take time to reset, even briefly, you're not just surviving your day—you're transforming it.

What Is Mindfulness, Really?

At its heart, mindfulness is the practice of being fully present in the moment. It's about focusing your attention on what's happening right now—internally and externally—without distraction or judgment. This might sound straightforward, but think about your average day. How often are you truly present?

You may find your thoughts drifting during a meeting, replaying a conversation from earlier or worrying about tomorrow's deadlines. Or maybe you're having dinner with loved ones, but instead of savoring the moment, your hand instinctively reaches for your phone. Sound familiar? These moments are the opposite of mindfulness—they're instances where we're physically present, but mentally somewhere else.

Mindfulness invites you to hit pause. It's like turning the volume down on the constant chatter in your mind. Imagine being able to tune out the noise and focus on what truly matters, whether it's the laughter of a friend, the aroma of your morning coffee, or the feel of the sun on your skin. It's a way to step out of autopilot and into awareness.

But here's the key: mindfulness isn't about achieving perfection. You don't need to maintain a Zen-like state of calm 24/7. Instead, it's about cultivating moments of intentional presence throughout your day. These moments might be fleeting—a deep breath before a meeting or a quiet reflection during your commute—but their impact can be profound.

For example, imagine sitting in traffic after a stressful day. Instead of letting frustration take over, you use those minutes to take a few deep breaths and notice your surroundings. The tension in your shoulders eases, your racing thoughts slow down, and suddenly, you've reclaimed a sense of calm amidst the chaos.

Mindfulness isn't a magic trick—it's a skill. Like any skill, it requires practice and patience. At first, your mind might resist, darting from one thought to the next. That's okay. The beauty of mindfulness is that every moment offers a fresh start. Each time your mind wanders, you can gently guide it back to the present.

The Science of Mindfulness

You might be wondering, "Can something as simple as mindfulness really make a difference?" The answer is a resounding yes—and science backs it up. While mindfulness might sound like a wellness buzzword, it's actually a practice grounded in decades of research. Studies have shown that even short bursts of mindfulness can significantly improve your mental and physical well-being.

For starters, mindfulness has been proven to reduce stress. When life feels overwhelming, our bodies often activate the "fight or flight" response, flooding our systems with stress hormones like cortisol. While this response is helpful in true emergencies, living in a constant state of stress can take a toll on our health, leading to anxiety, fatigue, and even chronic illnesses. Mindfulness interrupts this cycle by activating the body's "rest and digest" system, which promotes relaxation and helps reduce cortisol levels.

But that's not all. Mindfulness has been shown to sharpen focus and improve cognitive performance. In a study published in *Psychological Science*, participants who practiced mindfulness for just a few minutes each day reported a 30% increase in their ability to concentrate and complete tasks efficiently. Imagine the power of reclaiming that mental energy—tackling your to-do list with clarity and precision, rather than feeling scattered and overwhelmed.

Mindfulness also boosts emotional resilience. Regular practice enhances the brain's neuroplasticity—its ability to adapt and form new, healthier connections. This means that over time, mindfulness can help rewire your brain to respond to challenges with greater calm and clarity. Instead of reacting impulsively to stressful situations, you're more likely to pause, assess, and respond thoughtfully.

Even more compelling is mindfulness's ability to improve overall happiness. By helping you tune into the present moment, mindfulness reduces rumination about the past and worry about the future—two major culprits behind feelings of dissatisfaction. Research from the University of Massachusetts found that participants who engaged in mindfulness practices experienced an increase in overall life satisfaction and a decrease in symptoms of depression and anxiety.

And let's not forget the physical benefits. Mindfulness has been linked to lower blood pressure, improved sleep quality, and even a stronger immune system. By simply taking time to breathe and focus, you're not just calming your mind—you're supporting your body in profound ways.

The beauty of these scientific findings is that they confirm what many practitioners of mindfulness have known for centuries: small, intentional actions can lead to big changes. You don't need hours to experience the benefits. Even five minutes of focused breathing or mindful observation can set positive changes in motion.

So, the next time you find yourself questioning whether mindfulness is worth it, remember the science. Each mindful moment is like an investment in your well-being, paying dividends in focus, resilience, and peace of mind.

Making Mindfulness Work for You

Mindfulness doesn't require a yoga mat, a serene retreat, or an hour of uninterrupted time. It's a practice that can fit seamlessly into your everyday life, no matter how packed your schedule might be. The beauty of mindfulness is its flexibility—it's something you can do anywhere, anytime. The key is to start small and find ways to make it work for you.

Let's address a common misconception: mindfulness isn't about sitting cross-legged on the floor with your eyes closed. Sure, that works for some, but mindfulness can be just as effective in the middle of your daily hustle. It's about intentionally tuning in to the present moment, no matter where you are or what you're doing.

Imagine this: you're waiting in line at the grocery store. Instead of scrolling through your phone, you take a moment to focus on your breath. You notice the rhythm of your inhalations and exhalations, the feel of your feet on the floor, and the sounds around you. In that brief moment, you've transformed an ordinary situation into an opportunity for mindfulness.

Here are a few practical ways to incorporate mindfulness into your day:

- **Mindful Breathing:** This is one of the simplest yet most powerful mindfulness techniques. Wherever you are, take a moment to focus solely on your breath. Inhale deeply through your nose, hold it for a count of three, then exhale slowly through your mouth. Repeat this for a few breaths. It's like hitting a reset button for your mind. This practice is particularly helpful during moments of stress, as it signals to your body that it's time to relax.

- **Body Scanning:** You don't need a spa day to relax your body; a quick body scan can do wonders. Close your eyes and bring your attention to different parts of your body, starting from the top of your head and working down to your toes. Notice where you're holding tension, and consciously release it. This exercise not only helps you relax but also strengthens your awareness of how stress manifests physically.

- **Mindful Walking:** Walking isn't just about getting from point A to point B; it's an opportunity to be fully present. The next time you're walking—whether it's to your car or around your neighborhood—focus on the sensations of your feet meeting the ground. Notice the rhythm of your steps, the feel of the air on your skin, and the sights around you. It's a simple way to bring mindfulness into motion.

- **Gratitude Moments:** Take a minute to reflect on three things you're grateful for. They don't have to be big—maybe it's the warmth of your coffee, the sound of birds chirping outside, or a kind word from a friend. Gratitude shifts your perspective, reminding you of the good in your life, even on tough days.

- **Mindful Eating:** Instead of rushing through meals or multitasking, dedicate a few moments to truly savor your food. Pay attention to the colors, textures, and flavors. Chew slowly and notice how your body feels as you eat. It's not just about enjoying your meal—it's about giving your mind a chance to slow down and reset.

These practices aren't about perfection; they're about progress. You might not get it right every time, and that's okay. The beauty of mindfulness is that it meets you where you are. Even a few minutes of focused attention can make a difference, so start where you can and build from there.

By weaving mindfulness into your daily routines, you'll begin to notice its impact—not just in moments of calm, but in how you respond to stress, connect with others, and approach your day with intention. The key is consistency. The more you practice, the more natural it will feel, and the easier it will be to find those mindful moments, even in the midst of chaos.

Your Five-Minute Challenge

Now that you've explored the magic of mindfulness, it's time to put it into practice. But don't worry—you don't need to overhaul your entire routine or set aside hours every day. In fact, just five minutes is all it takes to start experiencing the benefits.

Why five minutes? Because it's small enough to feel manageable but significant enough to create real change. These quick, intentional moments can act as anchors, grounding you amidst life's chaos. Think of them as your personal reset buttons—little reminders that you have the power to pause, breathe, and find clarity no matter how hectic your day might be.

Here's your challenge: for the next seven days, dedicate just five minutes a day to mindfulness. Choose one practice from the list below, or mix and match throughout the week. The goal is to experiment, notice how you feel, and begin building a habit that works for you.

Day-by-Day Ideas for Your Five-Minute Practice

- **Day 1: Mindful Breathing:** Start simple. Find a quiet spot, close your eyes, and focus on your breath. Inhale deeply for a count of four, hold for four, then exhale for six. Repeat for five minutes. Notice how your body responds—perhaps your shoulders relax or your racing thoughts slow down.

- **Day 2: Gratitude Reflection:** Spend five minutes writing down three things you're grateful for. These don't have to be monumental; even small joys like the warmth of your morning coffee or a favorite song can make the list. Reflect on why these things matter to you and how they make you feel.

- **Day 3: Body Scan:** Sit or lie down comfortably and close your eyes. Bring your attention to your body, starting at the top of your head and moving slowly down to your toes. Notice any areas of tension or discomfort and visualize releasing them with each exhale.

- **Day 4: Mindful Observation:** Step outside or find a window with a view. Spend five minutes observing your surroundings. Look for details you might usually miss—the way the leaves move in the wind, the patterns of light and shadow, or the sounds around you.

- **Day 5: Mindful Eating:** Dedicate one meal or snack to mindful eating. Take your time to really experience the flavors, textures, and aromas of your food. Chew slowly, savoring each bite. Notice how this changes your appreciation of the meal.

- **Day 6: Mindful Walking:** Take a five-minute walk, focusing on the sensations of movement. Feel your feet meeting the ground, notice the rhythm of your steps, and pay attention to the sights and sounds around you. Let each step be a reminder to stay present.

- **Day 7: Reflection and Intention Setting:** Use this final day to reflect on your mindfulness journey. How did you feel before and after each practice? What worked well for you, and what felt challenging? Spend a few minutes setting an intention for how you'll continue incorporating mindfulness into your life.

Tracking Your Progress

Consider keeping a mindfulness journal to document your experience each day. Write down what practice you chose, how it made you feel, and any observations you had. Over time, this can become a valuable tool for understanding what works best for you and how mindfulness is impacting your life.

A Mindful Reminder

Remember, mindfulness isn't about perfection—it's about showing up for yourself, even if just for a few moments each day. Some days, you might find it easy to focus and feel the benefits immediately. Other days, your mind may wander or distractions might creep in. That's okay. What matters is that you keep trying. Each mindful moment you create is a step toward greater balance, clarity, and resilience.

So, are you ready to take the five-minute challenge? Your journey toward a calmer, more present life starts now.

Takeaway

Taking just five minutes to rest isn't a luxury—it's a necessity. These brief pauses allow your mind and body to reset, recharge, and prepare for what's next. Whether it's stepping away from a task, closing your eyes, or simply breathing deeply, a 5-minute rest is a small investment with big returns.

Start by carving out a few moments today to pause and rest. Notice how even this short break can shift your energy and perspective.

A 5-minute rest is even more powerful when paired with mindful breathing. In the next chapter, we'll explore simple breathing techniques that can help you calm your mind, reduce stress, and find balance in any moment.

Chapter Three

Breathing Techniques for Instant Calm

Breathing—it's the one thing we do every moment of every day, yet we rarely give it a second thought. But when life gets overwhelming, your breath can be your most reliable ally. Think of it as your body's built-in reset button. Whether you're stuck in traffic, about to give a presentation, or just trying to wind down after a long day, intentional breathing can calm your mind and restore your focus.

Take a moment to imagine this: you're caught in a whirlwind of stress, your thoughts racing and your heart pounding. Now, close your eyes and take a long, deep breath. Inhale through your nose, hold for a moment, and exhale slowly through your mouth. Feel the tension ease, your shoulders drop, and your mind clear. That's the power of mindful breathing.

In this chapter, we'll explore simple yet transformative techniques you can use anytime, anywhere, to bring instant calm and clarity to your day.

The Science of Breathing

Why does breathing matter so much? When you're stressed, your body activates its fight-or-flight response, flooding your system with adrenaline and cortisol. Your breathing becomes shallow, your muscles tense, and your heart races. It's your body preparing for battle—even if the "threat" is just an overflowing inbox or a traffic jam.

Intentional breathing does the opposite. It signals to your nervous system that it's safe to relax. Studies show that deep, controlled breaths lower your heart rate, reduce cortisol levels, and increase oxygen flow to the brain. The result? A calmer, more focused you.

Try This: Discover Your Breath Pattern

Before we dive into specific techniques, let's get to know your natural breathing rhythm. Sit comfortably and close your eyes. Place one hand on your chest and the other on your belly. Take a few normal breaths and notice which hand rises more.

If it's your chest, your breathing is shallow—a common pattern in stress. If it's your belly, you're already engaging your diaphragm, the powerhouse of deep, calming breaths. Don't worry if your chest dominates; the techniques below will help you shift to deeper, more restorative breathing.

Breathing Techniques to Try

1. Deep Belly Breathing

This is the foundation of all mindful breathing techniques. It's simple, soothing, and perfect for resetting your body in moments of stress.

- **How to Do It:** Sit or lie down comfortably. Place one hand on your chest and the other on your belly. Inhale deeply through your nose, allowing your belly to rise as your diaphragm expands. Exhale slowly through your mouth, feeling your belly fall.

- **Try This:** Imagine your breath as a wave rolling onto the shore. As you inhale, the wave swells; as you exhale, it gently recedes. Repeat for five breaths, noticing how your body begins to relax.

- **Real-Life Example:** Emily, a high school teacher juggling lesson plans, parent emails, and the unpredictable energy of thirty teenagers, often felt her nerves creeping up before the first bell rang. One particularly chaotic morning, the copier jammed, the coffee pot was empty, and the classroom felt like a pressure cooker. Emily slipped into an empty storage closet, closed her eyes, and placed a hand on her stomach. She inhaled deeply through her nose, imagining her breath filling a balloon just below her ribs. Slowly, she exhaled through her mouth, letting the tension drain from her body like air leaving that balloon. With each breath, she felt her shoulders drop, her heartbeat steady, and her thoughts clear. By the time she returned to her classroom, she wasn't just ready to face the day—she felt fully present, ready to connect with her students.

2. The 4-7-8 Technique

Known as the "relaxation breath," this technique is a favorite for winding down after a long day or easing into sleep.

- **How to Do It:** Inhale through your nose for a count of four. Hold your breath for a count of seven. Exhale slowly through your mouth for a count of eight. Repeat this cycle three to four times.

- **Why It Works:** The extended exhale activates your parasympathetic nervous system, which calms your body's stress response. It's like a lullaby for your nervous system.

- **Try This:** Picture yourself in a quiet, candlelit room. With each breath, imagine the flame flickering gently, steadying as your breathing slows. Feel your body unwind with each exhale.

- **Real-Life Example:** Raj, a freelance graphic designer, often found himself working late into the night, his mind buzzing with deadlines and the glow of his laptop screen. Despite his exhaustion, he would lie in bed staring at the ceiling, replaying the day's work and worrying about the next. One evening, frustrated by the cycle, Raj decided to try the 4-7-8 breathing technique a friend had recommended. He turned off his screens, dimmed the lights, and sat cross-legged on his bed. Closing his eyes, he inhaled deeply through his nose for four counts, held his breath for seven, and exhaled for a slow count of eight. At first, his thoughts still raced, but by the fourth cycle, he noticed his jaw unclenching, his heartbeat slowing, and his body softening into the mattress. The next thing he remembered was waking up to the soft morning light filtering through his blinds—his first uninterrupted sleep in weeks

3. Box Breathing

This structured technique is often used by Navy SEALs to stay calm and focused under pressure.

- **How to Do It:** Inhale through your nose for a count of four. Hold your breath for a count of four. Exhale through your mouth for a count of four. Hold your breath again for a count of four. Repeat this cycle four times.

- **Why It Works:** Box breathing creates a steady rhythm, helping to stabilize your mind and body. It's especially useful in high-stress situations.

- **Try This:** Picture drawing a square in your mind. Each side of the square represents a phase of your breath: inhale, hold, exhale, hold. Visualize completing the square with every cycle.

- **Real-Life Example:** Sarah, a project manager at a fast-paced marketing firm, sat in the conference room surrounded by colleagues debating over an overdue campaign. Tensions were high, voices overlapping, and Sarah felt her throat tightening as her turn to speak approached. She gripped her pen, her pulse quickening, and the words she'd rehearsed in her mind seemed to scatter. Discreetly, she began box breathing. Inhale for four. She pictured the clean, structured lines of a square forming in her mind. Hold for four. The edges of the box sharpened, grounding her. Exhale for four. Her shoulders softened. Hold for four. The room seemed to quiet as she repeated the pattern. By the time her name was called, Sarah's voice came steady and confident, her thoughts organized. She realized afterward that box breathing had done more than calm her nerves—it had restored her clarity in the heat of the moment.

4. Alternate Nostril Breathing

This technique balances your nervous system and promotes mental clarity. It's especially useful when transitioning between tasks or calming pre-event jitters.

- **How to Do It:** Sit comfortably and close your right nostril with your thumb. Inhale deeply through your left nostril. Close your left nostril with your ring finger, release your thumb, and exhale through your right nostril. Inhale through your right nostril, close it, and exhale through your left. Repeat for 5–10 cycles.

- **Why It Works:** By alternating nostrils, you balance the flow of oxygen to both hemispheres of the brain, fostering a sense of calm and focus.

- **Try This:**Imagine your breath as a pendulum, swinging gently from one side to the other. With each cycle, feel your mind becoming more balanced and centered.

- **Real-Life Example:** Marcus had spent weeks preparing for his dream job interview—studying the company, practicing responses, and ironing his suit to perfection. But as he sat in the waiting room, the confidence he'd built began to waver. His palms were clammy, his chest felt tight, and every passing second seemed to amplify his self-doubt. Remembering a breathing exercise his yoga instructor had taught him, Marcus decided to try alternate nostril breathing. He closed his eyes and subtly brought his thumb to his right nostril, inhaling deeply through the left. Switching sides, he exhaled through the right and repeated the pattern, imagining his breath as a pendulum swinging calmly back and forth. With each cycle, his racing thoughts slowed, replaced by a steady focus. By the time the receptionist called his name, Marcus stood up with a smile, his heartbeat steady and his mind clear, ready to let his preparation shine.

Reflect and Apply

- Reflect: Which breathing technique resonated with you the most? What did you notice about your body and mind as you practiced it?

- Apply: Choose one technique to use daily this week. Notice how it impacts your mood, energy, or focus.

- Expand: Think of a stressful moment in your daily routine. How might mindful breathing help you navigate it with greater ease?

Takeaway

Your breath is more than just a function—it's a tool, always available, to help you find calm, focus, and clarity. By incorporating these techniques into your day, you're not just managing stress—you're reclaiming control over how you feel and respond to life's challenges.

In the next chapter, we'll explore how grounding techniques can anchor you in the present, helping you find stability in moments of chaos.

Chapter Four

The Art of Mindful Observation

Life moves at lightning speed, and too often, we miss the world around us. We glance without seeing, rush without experiencing, and skim over the richness of the present moment. Mindful observation is your invitation to slow down, to notice the overlooked, and to connect with the beauty and detail of everyday life.

Imagine walking into your home after a long day. Instead of rushing to your next task, you pause. You notice the faint smell of coffee lingering in the air, the way the late-afternoon sunlight spills across the floor, the sound of your favorite chair creaking as you sit. This is the art of mindful observation—bringing your attention fully to what is, rather than what was or what will be. It's a way to ground yourself in the present while discovering joy in the ordinary.

Why Mindful Observation Matters

At its core, mindful observation is about more than simply noticing things—it's about learning to see with intention, curiosity, and presence. It's easy to fall into the rhythm of autopilot, where our days blur together in a stream of tasks and distractions. But when we pause to observe, we step out of that cycle and re-engage with the richness of life.

Breaking Free from Autopilot

Have you ever driven home and realized you don't remember the journey? Or scrolled through your phone only to find that an hour has disappeared? That's autopilot—a state where we're physically present but mentally disconnected. Mindful observation is like flipping a switch. It brings your awareness back to the present moment, interrupting the habits of mindless living.

When you truly observe, you create a sense of pause—a moment to breathe, to see, and to experience. You start to notice the details that were always there but hidden behind the rush. The way sunlight dances on water, the faint hum of distant traffic, or even the subtle emotions in a friend's voice. These details pull you back to life, one observation at a time.

Tapping Into Emotional Balance

Observation isn't just about seeing; it's about feeling. When you take the time to observe, you create space for your emotions to settle. Imagine this: you're overwhelmed with a hundred worries vying for your attention. Instead of pushing through, you step outside and look at the trees swaying in the wind. You notice the way the leaves flicker, their colors shifting between light and shadow. With every second you spend observing, your thoughts slow. What felt chaotic now feels manageable.

By anchoring yourself in the present, mindful observation helps you regulate your emotions, replacing overwhelm with calm. It's not about escaping your problems—it's about finding the clarity to face them with a steady mind.

Sharpening Your Focus

Observation is a muscle, and like any muscle, it gets stronger with use. When you practice noticing details in your environment, you train your brain to focus. This skill doesn't just apply to mindfulness; it carries over to every aspect of your life.

Think about the last time you struggled to focus on a task. Your mind wandered, distractions crept in, and productivity stalled. Now imagine how sharper observation could change that. By learning to notice details, you strengthen your ability to concentrate—on a project, a conversation, or even a challenging moment.

Building Deeper Connections

Mindful observation isn't limited to objects or nature—it's also a powerful tool for connecting with others. How often do we miss the subtle cues that reveal what someone is really feeling? A flicker of worry in their eyes, a pause before they speak, or the way their hands fidget as they talk.

When you truly observe someone, you're saying: "I see you. I'm here." This kind of attention deepens relationships, building trust and empathy. It's the difference between hearing someone's words and understanding their heart.

For example, imagine your partner is unusually quiet after work. Instead of brushing it off, you notice the tension in their posture and the way they sigh after speaking. By gently asking, "You seem like you've had a tough day—want to talk about it?" you create a space for connection. That small act of observation can turn a moment of distance into one of closeness.

Discovering Beauty in the Ordinary

One of the greatest gifts of mindful observation is rediscovering the beauty in what you once overlooked. A cup of tea isn't just a drink—it's steam rising in soft tendrils, warmth cradling your hands, and a quiet moment of comfort. A walk isn't just exercise—it's the crunch of leaves underfoot, the rhythm of your steps, and the way the light filters through the trees.

When you observe with intention, even the simplest things take on new meaning. You start to realize that life's richness isn't hidden in grand moments—it's woven into the fabric of everyday existence.

Techniques for Mindful Observation

1. The One-Minute Observation Challenge

- **How to Do It:** Choose an object—a flower, a coffee cup, or a book. Spend one full minute observing it closely. Notice its color, texture, size, and shape. Resist the urge to label or analyze. Simply notice what's there.

- **Expanded Real-Life Example:** Rachel sat on her porch one morning, coffee in hand and to-do list looming in her mind. Feeling overwhelmed, she set a timer for one minute and focused on the tree across the yard. At first, it was just a tree—a tangle of branches and leaves. But as she looked closer, she noticed the intricate network of veins in the leaves, the soft sway of the branches in the breeze, and the play of light and shadow across the bark. She was struck by its quiet strength, standing tall through storms and seasons. By the time the timer buzzed, Rachel felt calmer, her mental clutter replaced by a sense of grounding and peace.

2. Observing in Nature

- **How to Do It:** Take a short walk outdoors. Pause to focus on one element of your surroundings—like the sound of birds, the feel of the wind, or the pattern of leaves. Let your senses guide you, noticing new details as you move.

- **Expanded Real-Life Example:** After a particularly stressful day at work, Andre took a walk along his neighborhood trail, head-phones left behind for once. As he walked, he noticed the gravel crunching under his shoes, the faint scent of pine in the air, and the distant hum of a lawnmower. He stopped at a small pond he usually passed without a glance and crouched down, noticing ripples on the surface as a dragonfly hovered nearby. For the first time in weeks, he felt the weight of his stress lifting, replaced by a quiet appreciation for the small, vibrant details of the natural world.

3. Observing Emotions in Others

- **How to Do It:** During a conversation, pay attention to the other person's facial expressions, gestures, and tone of voice. Notice what they're feeling beyond their words. Respond with curiosity, saying: "It sounds like this has been really challenging. How are you feeling now?"

- **Expanded Real-Life Example:** Maya's teenage son had been unusually quiet during dinner. Instead of jumping in with ques-tions, she observed his body language—the way he hunched his shoulders and stared at his plate. Gently, she said, "You seem a little off tonight. Want to talk about what's on your mind?" He looked up, his eyes filling with tears as he shared a tough moment from his day. By tuning in to his subtle cues, Maya had created a safe space for him to open up, deepening their connection in a way that words alone never could have achieved.

4. Observing Your Daily Tasks

- **How to Do It:** Pick a simple task, like making coffee or folding laundry. Focus on the sensations involved: the smell of the coffee, the texture of the fabric, the rhythm of your movements. Let the act itself become your anchor to the present moment.

- **Expanded Real-Life Example:** David approached laundry as a chore to rush through—until one evening when he decided to practice mindful observation. As he folded each shirt, he noticed the softness of the fabric, the faint scent of lavender from the detergent, and the satisfying crispness of a well-made fold. He realized that even this mundane task carried a quiet rhythm, a chance to slow down and find calm amidst the noise of daily life. By the time he finished, he felt surprisingly centered, as though he'd meditated without even trying.

Reflection Prompts

- When was the last time you truly observed your surroundings? What details stood out to you?

- Which of these techniques feels most natural to try?

- How might mindful observation change the way you approach your relationships, work, or daily routines?

Takeaway

Mindful observation is more than a technique—it's a way of seeing the world. By tuning into the details around you, you can break free from autopilot mode and rediscover the beauty in the ordinary. Whether you're observing the intricate patterns of nature, the subtle emotions of a loved one, or the simple act of folding a towel, each moment of awareness is an opportunity to ground yourself, find clarity, and deepen your connection to life.

In the next chapter, we'll explore visualization—another powerful tool for shifting your mindset and unlocking your potential.

Chapter Five

Quick Visualization Exercises

Your mind is a powerful tool. What you imagine can shape how you feel, act, and respond to the world around you. Visualization is the practice of creating mental images to guide your thoughts and emotions in a positive direction.

Athletes use visualization to mentally rehearse their performances, seeing themselves crossing the finish line or scoring the winning goal. This same tool can help you prepare for challenges, boost your confidence, and bring calm to overwhelming moments.

Why Visualization Works

Visualization is more than daydreaming—it's a powerful mental tool that taps into your brain's natural ability to create, process, and adapt. When you visualize, you're not just imagining a scenario; you're training your mind and body to respond as if it's real. This practice bridges the gap between where you are and where you want to be, making it a cornerstone of mindfulness, personal growth, and resilience.

The Brain's Power to Simulate Reality

Here's the fascinating part: your brain doesn't distinguish much between what you vividly imagine and what you actually experience. When you picture yourself confidently delivering a speech, running through a lush forest, or sitting peacefully by the ocean, your brain activates the same neural pathways as if you were physically there.

This is why athletes mentally rehearse crossing the finish line or scoring the winning goal. It's not wishful thinking—it's preparation. Visualization primes your brain and body for the real thing, building muscle memory and emotional readiness.

Take Serena, a marathon runner. On the eve of her races, she would close her eyes and visualize herself gliding across the finish line, her legs steady and her breath rhythmic. By the time the race day arrived, her mind already "knew" what success felt like, giving her the confidence to perform at her best.

Shifting Your Emotional State

Visualization doesn't just prepare you for the future—it can transform how you feel in the moment. Imagine you're overwhelmed by stress, your thoughts spinning in a hundred directions. Now close your eyes and picture yourself standing by a serene lake, the water still and glassy, reflecting a clear blue sky. As you breathe, you imagine your stress dissolving into the air like mist. Your shoulders relax, your heart rate slows, and your mind feels lighter.

This shift isn't magic; it's science. Visualization activates the parasympathetic nervous system—the "rest and digest" mode of your body—helping to calm anxiety and restore balance. It's like giving your brain a reset button, allowing you to step back into the moment with clarity and control.

Reinforcing Confidence and Resilience

Visualization also plays a key role in reshaping your self-image. When you imagine yourself succeeding—nailing a presentation, having a productive day, or responding gracefully to a challenge—you're reinforcing a belief in your own capabilities. Over time, this mental rehearsal strengthens your confidence and builds emotional resilience.

Take Ben, for example, who struggled with self-doubt before job interviews. Instead of letting his nerves take over, he began visualizing himself walking into the interview room with calm assurance, answering questions with clarity, and leaving with a sense of accomplishment. By the time the real interviews came, he wasn't just hoping for success—he had already experienced it in his mind.

The Science of Neuroplasticity

Your brain is constantly adapting and rewiring itself—a phenomenon known as neuroplasticity. Visualization leverages this adaptability by creating and strengthening neural pathways associated with positive behaviors, thoughts, and emotions.

Consider this: if you repeatedly imagine yourself reacting calmly in high-pressure situations, you're training your brain to default to calmness when those situations arise. Over time, visualization becomes a tool for rewiring habitual responses, helping you move from reactivity to intentionality.

Making the Subconscious Your Ally

Your subconscious mind is a powerful force—it shapes your beliefs, drives your habits, and influences your decisions in ways you may not even realize. Visualization acts as a bridge to your subconscious, planting seeds of possibility and empowerment.

For instance, if you visualize yourself achieving a goal—say, writing a book—you're not just imagining the outcome. You're sending a message to your subconscious that this goal is possible and worth pursuing. This subtle shift in mindset can help you stay motivated, spot opportunities, and overcome obstacles along the way.

Unlocking Creativity and Problem-Solving

Sometimes, visualization isn't about calming your mind or building confidence—it's about unlocking your creativity. When you picture solutions, explore "what if" scenarios, or imagine yourself in a different perspective, you activate your brain's creative centers.

Emily, an artist facing a creative block, used visualization to reignite her imagination. She would close her eyes and picture herself walking through an enchanted forest, the colors vivid and the air alive with possibility. This exercise helped her reconnect with her sense of wonder, inspiring new ideas for her work.

Techniques to Try

1. Calm Oasis Visualization

What It Does: Grounds you during moments of stress by creating a mental escape.

How to Do It:

- Close your eyes and take a few deep breaths.

- Picture a place that feels calming and safe—perhaps a beach, a forest, or a cozy room.

- Imagine the sights, sounds, and textures of this place: the warmth of the sun, the rustle of leaves, or the feel of soft blankets.

- Stay in this mental oasis for 1–2 minutes, letting your body relax as you focus on the imagery.

2. Future-Self Visualization

What It Does: Builds confidence and motivates you to align with your goals.

How to Do It:

- Think about a specific goal or challenge you want to overcome.

- Close your eyes and imagine your future self successfully achieving it.

- Visualize every detail: What are you doing? How do you feel? What's happening around you?

- Let this image inspire you to take the next step toward your goal.

3. Preparing for a Challenging Conversation

What It Does: Reduces anxiety and improves your approach to high-stakes discussions.

How to Do It:

- Before the conversation, close your eyes and picture the setting: where you'll be, who you'll talk to, and how the discussion will unfold.

- Imagine yourself speaking calmly and confidently, expressing your points clearly.

- Visualize the other person responding thoughtfully and the conversation ending positively.

4. Visualization for Overcoming Obstacles

What It Does: Encourages resilience and a problem-solving mindset.

How to Do It:

- Think of a current challenge or obstacle in your life.

- Visualize yourself moving through the difficulty with grace and determination.

- Picture solutions emerging and how you feel once the obstacle is resolved.

5. Visualization with Movement

What It Does: Combines physical action with mental imagery to enhance focus and calm.

How to Do It:

- Choose a repetitive movement, like walking or stretching.

- As you move, imagine energy flowing through your body, bringing relaxation with each step or stretch.

- Picture stress leaving your body as you exhale and focus on the rhythm of your movements.

A Mindful Moment: Bella's Story

Bella had always dreaded public speaking. Before every presentation, she felt the familiar wave of nausea and self-doubt. Then a colleague introduced her to visualization.

The night before her next presentation, Bella closed her eyes and pictured herself standing confidently in front of her audience. She imagined the sound of her voice steady and clear, the nods of understanding from her listeners, and the sense of accomplishment afterward.

When the moment came, Bella still felt nervous, but the visualization had prepared her. She delivered her talk with more ease than ever before, and the positive response reinforced her confidence.

Reflect and Apply

- **Reflect:** What situations in your life feel most stressful? How might visualization help you approach them differently?

- **Apply:** Choose one visualization exercise from this chapter to practice today. Start with a small scenario, like calming yourself during a hectic morning or preparing for a task.

- **Expand:** Try a different visualization technique each day for a week, noting which ones resonate most with you.

Takeaway

Visualization is a simple yet powerful way to reset your mind, calm your emotions, and prepare for success. By imagining positive outcomes or creating mental escapes, you can train your brain to approach challenges with confidence and clarity.

Another powerful way to reset your mind is by cultivating gratitude. Gratitude journaling shifts your focus from what's going wrong to what's going right, helping you build resilience and joy even on the busiest days. In the next chapter, we'll explore how this simple practice can transform your mindset.

Chapter Six

The 5-Minute Gratitude Journal

Life can feel like a whirlwind of demands, setbacks, and stressors, leaving little room to pause and reflect. It's tempting to focus on the negatives—the missed opportunities, the delays, the chaos—and that focus can become all-consuming. But what if, instead of being swept away by what's wrong, you could anchor yourself in what's right?

This is where gratitude steps in. Gratitude is the practice of shifting your attention from what's lacking to what's present, from what's troubling to what's uplifting. It's not about denying life's challenges; it's about noticing the moments of light that still shine through the clouds.

Think about this: when was the last time you felt truly grateful? Maybe it was a kind word from a stranger, the warmth of the sun on your face, or the comfort of a friend who listened without judgment. In that moment, did you notice how your perspective softened? How your heart felt a little lighter? That's the power of gratitude.

The Science of Gratitude

Gratitude isn't just a feel-good buzzword—it's backed by science. Research has shown that cultivating gratitude can lower stress, improve sleep, enhance relationships, and even boost your immune system. How? Gratitude rewires your brain, training it to notice and appreciate the positives in your life.

When you practice gratitude regularly, you activate the brain's reward centers, releasing feel-good neurotransmitters like dopamine and serotonin. Over time, this practice can reduce the brain's natural negativity bias, the tendency to focus on threats or problems. Gratitude acts like a mental filter, helping you see more of the good and less of the bad.

For example, a study conducted by the University of California, Davis, found that participants who kept a gratitude journal for just three weeks reported higher levels of optimism, better physical health, and stronger emotional well-being. The researchers concluded that even small, consistent acts of gratitude could have a profound and lasting impact.

Why 5 Minutes Is Enough

You don't need hours to experience the benefits of gratitude. Even five minutes a day can make a difference. Think of it like watering a plant—you don't have to drench it, but consistent, small doses help it thrive. In the same way, brief moments of focused gratitude nourish your mindset, creating resilience and joy that grow over time.

Imagine ending each day with a simple ritual: opening your journal, writing down three things that brought you joy, and reflecting on why they mattered. It might be the aroma of fresh coffee in the morning, a kind text from a friend, or the satisfaction of completing a small task.

These aren't grand gestures—they're tiny treasures, reminders that even in the busiest or hardest days, good things exist.

This practice doesn't require perfect circumstances or ideal conditions. In fact, it's most powerful during difficult times, when gratitude feels hardest to find. Like a candle in the dark, gratitude shines brightest in moments of challenge.

A Story of Gratitude in Action

Mia had always been a glass-half-empty kind of person. She'd dwell on her frustrations—her boss's unreasonable deadlines, her cluttered apartment, her missed workout. One evening, after venting to a friend, she was challenged to try a gratitude journal. Skeptical but willing, Mia grabbed an old notebook and started small:

1. Her cat curling up in her lap.

2. The warmth of her tea.

3. A funny joke she'd heard that day.

At first, it felt forced, even trivial. But as the days passed, Mia noticed something remarkable. She started scanning her day for "gratitude moments," noticing small pleasures she'd previously ignored. A stranger holding the elevator door. The golden light of sunset streaming through her window. The sound of rain tapping gently against the glass. Six months later, Mia's gratitude journal was full, and so was her heart.

Gratitude didn't erase her challenges, but it gave her the strength and perspective to face them.

Your Gratitude Journey Starts Here

In this chapter, we'll explore how to start your own 5-minute gratitude journal, complete with simple prompts, reflection exercises, and strategies to deepen your practice. Whether you're new to gratitude or looking to expand your existing practice, you'll discover that these small moments of intentional reflection can transform not only your day but your outlook on life.

Gratitude is an invitation—to slow down, to notice, and to appreciate. In just five minutes, you can take that first step toward a more grounded, joyful, and resilient life. Let's begin.

Gratitude During Tough Times

It's easy to feel grateful when life is going well, but what about when it's not? Gratitude during challenging times isn't about ignoring hardships—it's about finding small moments of hope, strength, or connection that help you move forward.

For example:

- A kind word from a colleague on a stressful day.

- The warmth of a hot cup of tea when you're feeling overwhelmed.

- A sunset that reminds you of the beauty in the world.

Gratitude doesn't erase struggles, but it can shift your focus, giving you the strength to keep going.

How to Start Your Gratitude Journal

1. The 3-Item Rule

What It Does: Keeps the practice simple and sustainable.

How to Do It:

- Each day, write down three things you're grateful for.

- Be specific: Instead of "I'm grateful for my family," try "I'm grateful for the laugh I shared with my sister over dinner."

2. Gratitude in the Moment

What It Does: Helps you notice gratitude in real time.

How to Do It:

- Throughout your day, pause when you notice something positive—a kind gesture, a beautiful scene, or a moment of peace.

- Take a mental snapshot of the moment, savoring how it makes you feel.

3. Reflective Gratitude

What It Does: Helps you find gratitude in challenges.

How to Do It:

- Think of a difficult experience you've faced recently.

- Ask yourself: What did I learn from it? Who supported me during this time? What small moments of comfort or kindness helped me through?

- Write down your reflections in your journal.

Reflect and Apply

- **Reflect**: When was the last time you felt truly grateful? How did that moment change your outlook?

- **Apply**: Start your gratitude journal today by writing down three things you're thankful for. Choose a time that works for you—morning, evening, or a quiet moment in between.

- **Challenge**: For the next week, practice gratitude in a challenging situation. Write about one positive thing that emerges, even if it's small.

Takeaway

Gratitude is like a muscle—the more you use it, the stronger it becomes. By dedicating just five minutes a day to focusing on the good in your life, you can create a ripple effect of positivity, resilience, and joy.

Gratitude helps center your thoughts, but sometimes, life's demands pull you in many directions at once. When your mind feels scattered, grounding techniques can anchor you in the present moment. Let's discover how these simple exercises can help you stay calm and focused.

Chapter Seven

Grounding Techniques for Busy Minds

In the fast-paced shuffle of daily life, it's easy to feel unmoored—like your thoughts are racing faster than you can catch them, pulling you in a dozen directions at once. The notifications ping, the to-do list grows, and before you know it, your body is here, but your mind is somewhere else entirely.

Grounding techniques offer a way to press pause. They help you anchor yourself in the present moment, pulling your attention away from the endless swirl of thoughts and bringing it back to what's tangible, steady, and real. Imagine standing in the middle of a storm with a rope securely tied to a strong tree. That rope is grounding—it keeps you from being swept away.

Think about your busiest moments: rushing through an airport, fielding back-to-back meetings, or managing a house full of energetic kids. Those are the moments when grounding becomes invaluable. It doesn't require hours of meditation or perfect calm; it's something you can do in seconds to steady your mind and regain control.

Grounding is about coming back to your senses—literally. By focusing on what you can see, hear, feel, smell, or taste, you shift your attention from the whirlwind in your mind to the solid, present reality of your body and environment. And from that place of stability, you can face whatever comes next.

Why Grounding Works

When your mind is scattered or overwhelmed, it's like a computer with too many tabs open—slow, inefficient, and prone to freezing up. Grounding techniques act as a hard reset, helping you close those mental tabs and refocus your attention.

Reconnecting with Your Body

Stress often pulls you out of your body and into your head. You start overthinking, replaying conversations, or worrying about future outcomes. This mental overdrive disconnects you from the physical sensations of the present moment—the solid floor beneath your feet, the steady rhythm of your breath, or the warmth of sunlight on your skin.

Grounding works by flipping the script. Instead of letting your thoughts lead, it invites your body to take the wheel. By paying attention to physical sensations, you interrupt the stress cycle and remind your brain that you're here, you're safe, and you're in control.

Imagine this: you're sitting in your car after a long, stressful day, your heart racing and your thoughts spiraling. You take a deep breath and focus on the texture of the steering wheel under your hands, the gentle hum of the engine, and the smell of rain on the pavement. In that moment, your scattered mind starts to settle. You're no longer drowning in stress—you're anchored.

Calming the Nervous System

Grounding techniques engage the parasympathetic nervous system—the part of your body responsible for rest and relaxation. When stress triggers your fight-or-flight response, your heart races, your muscles tense, and your body floods with adrenaline. Grounding interrupts this cycle, signaling to your brain that the danger has passed.

This isn't just theory; it's biology. Research shows that grounding practices can lower cortisol levels, reduce blood pressure, and even regulate heart rate variability—physical markers of stress reduction.

For example, a study on the 5-4-3-2-1 technique (naming sensory inputs) found that participants reported a significant decrease in anxiety after just five minutes of practice. By tuning into their senses, they were able to shift their focus from internal worries to external realities, creating a sense of calm and control.

Creating Mental Space

Grounding isn't just about calming down—it's about making space for clarity. When your mind is caught in a loop of worry or overwhelm, it's hard to think clearly or solve problems effectively. Grounding techniques help you clear the mental fog, so you can approach challenges with a fresh perspective.

Take Priya, a college student preparing for finals. After hours of cramming, she felt her anxiety skyrocketing, her thoughts jumping from one subject to the next. She stepped outside and practiced a simple grounding exercise: barefoot walking on the grass. As she felt the cool blades under her feet and the soft earth beneath, her breathing slowed, and her mind quieted. When she returned to her studies, she felt not only calmer but sharper and more focused.

Building Resilience Over Time

The beauty of grounding is that it's both immediate and cumulative. In the moment, it helps you find stability and calm. Over time, regular grounding practices build resilience, making it easier to navigate future stressors without feeling overwhelmed.

It's like strengthening a muscle. The more you practice grounding, the quicker and more naturally your mind and body will return to balance. You start to develop an internal compass—a steadying force you can rely on, no matter what life throws your way.

Your First Step

Grounding doesn't require anything fancy—just a willingness to pause and tune in. In the next section, we'll explore practical techniques you can use anytime, anywhere, to anchor yourself and regain clarity. Whether it's connecting with your senses, focusing on your breath, or using nature as a grounding tool, you'll discover that a calmer, steadier mind is always within reach.

Techniques to Try

1. The 5-4-3-2-1 Technique

What It Does: Anchors you in the present by engaging your senses.

How to Do It:

- Look around and name:

- 5 things you can see.

- 4 things you can touch.

- 3 things you can hear.

- 2 things you can smell.

- 1 thing you can taste.

- Take your time, noticing details and textures to fully engage your senses.

2. Weighted Grounding

What It Does: Uses physical pressure to promote a sense of stability and calm.

How to Do It:

- Hold a weighted object, like a blanket or beanbag, or place a pillow on your lap.

- Focus on the sensation of weight and how it connects you to your surroundings.

- Breathe deeply, imagining tension leaving your body with each exhale.

3. Grounding Through Texture

What It Does: Provides tactile input to anchor your focus during anxiety.

How to Do It:

- Keep a grounding object, like a smooth stone, textured fabric, or a stress ball, nearby.

- Run your fingers over it, focusing on the texture and how it feels in your hand.

- Let the sensation anchor your attention and steady your thoughts.

4. Grounding in Public Settings

What It Does: Helps you find calm in high-stress environments, like airports or meetings.

How to Do It:

- Focus on something neutral in your surroundings, like the pattern on a wall, the sound of footsteps, or the texture of a chair.

- Inhale deeply for a count of four, then exhale slowly for a count of six.

- Repeat until your thoughts settle, letting your surroundings bring you back to the moment.

5. Nature Dased Grounding

What It Does: Connects you to the natural world, promoting calm and clarity.

How to Do It:

- Step outside and place your bare feet on the grass, dirt or sand.

- Notice the texture and temperature beneath your feet.

- Breathe deeply, imagining yourself rooted to the earth.

A Mindful Moment: Jason's Story

Jason had always been a worrier, but juggling a demanding job and a toddler at home left him feeling constantly frazzled. One day, after a particularly tense meeting, he felt his anxiety spike—his heart raced, and his thoughts spiraled.

Instead of pushing through, Jason tried the 5-4-3-2-1 technique a friend had mentioned. Naming five things in his office—the blue pen on his desk, the ticking clock—helped slow his mind. By the time he reached "one thing he could taste" (his coffee), Jason felt steady enough to move on with his day.

Grounding didn't eliminate Jason's stress, but it gave him the tools to pause, reset, and approach challenges with clarity.

Reflect and Apply

- **Reflect**: Think about a recent moment when you felt over-whelmed or scattered. How could grounding techniques have helped you anchor yourself in that moment?

- **Apply**: Choose one of the techniques from this chapter today. Notice how it changes your mood or focus.

- **Expand**: Experiment with a grounding technique in different set-tings—at home, at work, or outdoors. Which works best for you?

Takeaway

Grounding techniques are life skills, not just quick fixes. They anchor you during chaos, helping you regain balance and clarity. Whether it's connecting with your senses, using nature for calm, or using texture for focus, grounding offers a reliable way to find stability, no matter what's happening around you.

Grounding brings you back to the present, and affirmations empower you to shape your inner dialogue. By focusing on intentional, positive statements, you can rewrite the narrative in your mind and cultivate self-confidence and purpose. Let's dive into the transformative power of affirmations.

Chapter Eight

The Power of Affirmations

What does your inner voice sound like? For many of us, it's not always the kindest. It whispers doubts when we're about to take a risk, replays embarrassing moments when we want to move forward, and amplifies fears during our quietest moments. Over time, this inner critic can shape how we see ourselves, holding us back from the life we want to live.

But what if you could rewrite that script? What if, instead of a voice that undermines, you cultivated one that uplifts? This is the power of affirmations—a tool for intentionally shaping your inner dialogue to reflect your strength, goals, and potential.

Affirmations are more than just positive words; they're a declaration of possibility. When repeated with intention and belief, they become a roadmap for the person you want to be and the life you want to create. Think of affirmations as planting seeds in the fertile soil of your subconscious. With consistent care and attention, those seeds grow into beliefs, behaviors, and habits that align with your values and aspirations.

Imagine starting each day with affirmations like:

- "I am capable of handling whatever comes my way."

50

- "I am growing into the best version of myself."

- "I deserve kindness, respect, and success."

Over time, these statements become more than words. They become truths. Affirmations don't just describe who you are—they guide you toward who you're becoming.

Why Affirmations Work

At first glance, affirmations might seem too simple to make a difference. But beneath their simplicity lies a profound psychological and neurological impact. Affirmations work because they directly address the thoughts and patterns that shape your reality.

Rewiring Your Brain

Your brain is a creature of habit, constantly building and reinforcing neural pathways based on your thoughts and behaviors. If you often think, "I'm not good enough," your brain strengthens that pathway, making the thought easier to return to in the future. It's like a well-worn trail through a forest the more you walk it, the clearer it becomes.

Affirmations carve out new trails. When you say, "I am capable and confident," you're signaling to your brain to form a new pathway—one that focuses on your potential rather than your limitations. Over time, these positive pathways grow stronger, while the old, negative trails fade into the background.

This process, called neuroplasticity, is the brain's ability to adapt and change. It's the same mechanism that allows you to learn new skills, break bad habits, and develop healthier thought patterns. Affirmations are a way to consciously direct this process, guiding your brain toward beliefs that empower and support you.

Shifting Your Emotional State

Have you ever noticed how your thoughts shape your emotions? A negative thought can trigger a cascade of anxiety or self-doubt, while a positive thought can inspire calm or confidence. Affirmations harness this connection, allowing you to shift your emotional state with intentional focus.

For example, imagine you're about to give a big presentation, and your mind is flooded with thoughts like, "I'm going to mess this up." Instead of spiraling, you pause and repeat: "I am prepared. I am confident. I am ready to succeed." At first, it might feel forced, but with each repetition, you notice your shoulders relaxing, your breathing steadying, and your confidence growing.

Affirmations act as emotional anchors, reminding you of your strengths when doubt threatens to pull you under. They're a way of choosing your mindset, even in challenging moments.

Boosting Self-Efficacy

Self-efficacy is the belief in your ability to influence outcomes—a cornerstone of confidence and resilience. Affirmations reinforce this belief by focusing your attention on what's possible rather than what's problematic.

Take Clara, a new entrepreneur navigating the uncertainties of starting her own business. Each morning, she repeats affirmations like, "I have the skills to create success," and "I am capable of overcoming challenges." These statements don't magically eliminate obstacles, but they remind her of her ability to tackle them. Over time, Clara notices a shift: she approaches setbacks with curiosity rather than fear, seeing them as opportunities to learn and grow.

Engaging Your Subconscious Mind

Your subconscious mind is like a sponge, soaking up the messages you expose it to—whether positive or negative. The thoughts you repeat become the framework through which your subconscious operates, influencing your decisions, behaviors, and outlook.

Affirmations allow you to take control of that process, planting intentional messages that align with your goals. When you consistently repeat, "I am worthy of success," your subconscious begins to internalize it as fact, shaping your actions and decisions to reflect that belief.

For instance, Alex, who struggled with imposter syndrome in his tech job, began using affirmations to challenge his doubts. He repeated, "I bring unique value to my team," and "My contributions are meaningful." Over time, he found himself speaking up more in meetings, taking on leadership roles, and trusting his instincts. The affirmations didn't just change how Alex thought—they changed how he showed up in his work.

A Tool for Resilience

Life is full of ups and downs, and affirmations don't promise to eliminate challenges. What they do offer is a tool for resilience—a way to ground yourself in hope, strength, and possibility, even in difficult times.

Consider Maria, who faced a tough breakup. In the weeks that followed, she felt lost and unsure of herself. To rebuild, she started each day with affirmations like, "I am whole on my own," and "Each day, I grow stronger." The affirmations didn't erase her grief, but they reminded her of her inner strength, helping her navigate the healing process with grace and self-compassion.

Your Affirmation Practice Begins Here

In the next sections, we'll explore how to craft powerful affirmations that resonate deeply with your goals and values. You'll learn practical ways to integrate them into your daily routine—whether it's during your morning coffee, your commute, or moments of reflection.

Affirmations aren't just words; they're declarations of your potential. With each repetition, you're taking a step closer to the life you want to create. Let's get started.

Creating Affirmations That Stick

Not all affirmations are created equal. The most effective ones are personal, specific, and aligned with your values and goals.

Guidelines for Crafting Affirmations

1. **Keep Them Positive**: Focus on what you want to achieve, not what you want to avoid.

   - Instead of: "I won't fail," try: "I am capable of success."

1. **Make Them Believable**: Choose statements that feel authentic and achievable.

   - Instead of: "I am fearless," try: "I am learning to approach challenges with courage."

1. **Use Present Tense**: Speak as if the affirmation is already true to reinforce your belief.

   - Example: "I am calm and confident in stressful situations."

1. **Tailor Them to Specific Contexts**: Affirmations are most effec-

tive when they address a particular need or challenge in your life.

Examples of Context-Specific Affirmations

1. Work Stress

- "I handle challenges at work with focus and composure."

- "I am valued for my contributions."

- "I am capable of finding creative solutions to problems."

2. Self-Esteem

- "I deserve kindness and respect from myself and others."

- "I am proud of who I am becoming."

- "I release the need for perfection and embrace progress."

3. Relationships

- "I communicate with honesty and compassion."

- "I attract healthy, supportive relationships into my life."

- "I am grateful for the love and connection in my life."

Techniques to Amplify Your Affirmations

1. Morning Affirmations

Start your day by repeating affirmations that set a positive tone. Pair them with a calming routine, like sipping tea or doing light stretches.

2. Affirmations with Visualization

Combine affirmations with mental imagery to make them more vivid.

- Example: If you're affirming, "I am confident in presentations," visualize yourself delivering a speech with ease and receiving positive feedback.

3. Written Affirmations

Write your affirmations daily in a journal to reinforce their impact. Use colorful pens or creative layouts to make the practice enjoyable.

4. Anchoring Affirmations to Habits

Pair affirmations with everyday routines to make them automatic. For example:

- Repeat affirmations while brushing your teeth, driving, or taking a shower.

5. Affirmations with Movement

Engage your body while repeating affirmations to enhance their emotional resonance.

- As you walk, sync each step with a phrase like: "I am moving forward with strength."

- During yoga or stretching, match affirmations to your breath or movements.

A Mindful Moment: Elena's Story

Elena struggled with self-doubt in her new role as a team leader. After a particularly challenging meeting, she felt overwhelmed and unsure of her abilities. A mentor suggested affirmations to help her reframe her mindset.

Each morning, Elena stood in front of her mirror, placed her hands on her hips in a power pose, and repeated:

- "I am capable of leading with clarity and compassion."

- "I trust myself to make thoughtful decisions."

- "I am learning and growing every day."

At first, the practice felt awkward. But over time, Elena noticed a shift. She approached her team meetings with greater confidence and found herself focusing on solutions instead of fears. Affirmations became her anchor, reminding her of her strengths when doubts crept in.

Reflect and Apply

- **Reflect**: What limiting beliefs or negative thoughts do you often replay in your mind? How might affirmations help you reframe these patterns?

- **Apply**: Choose one area of your life—work, relationships, or self-esteem—and craft three affirmations specific to that context. Practice repeating them daily for a week.

- **Challenge**: Pair your affirmations with another mindfulness practice, like visualization or journaling. Reflect on how this combination enhances your mindset.

Takeaway

Affirmations are more than words—they're declarations of possibility and intention. By weaving them into your daily routine, you can rewire your brain, shift your mindset, and cultivate greater confidence and self-belief.

With affirmations as a key tool in your mindfulness practice, the next step is to bring everything together into a cohesive system. In the final chapter, you'll learn how to build a personalized mindfulness toolkit that empowers you to reset and recharge anytime, anywhere.

Chapter Nine

Movement Breaks for Mental Clarity

We've all been there: you're stuck at your desk, staring at the same sentence, spreadsheet, or email draft for what feels like forever. Your brain feels sluggish, your focus has vanished, and every small task suddenly feels monumental. So what do you do? Push harder? Sip another cup of coffee? Scroll your phone for a "break" that somehow leaves you feeling even more drained?

Here's a better idea: move

Movement isn't just for fitness—it's a mental reset, a way to clear the cobwebs and reignite your focus. Even just a few minutes of intentional movement can refresh your mind, boost your creativity, and help you tackle your day with renewed clarity. Think of it as a power nap for your brain, but without the groggy wake-up.

Imagine this: you're in the middle of a long workday, and your energy hits rock bottom. Instead of slogging through, you stand up, stretch your arms to the ceiling, and take a brisk walk around the block. The fresh air sharpens your senses, your muscles loosen, and suddenly, that impossible task seems doable again. This is the magic of movement—it shifts your energy, both physically and mentally, helping you return to your work with a clearer head and a lighter heart.

In this chapter, we'll explore how simple, accessible movement breaks can transform your productivity and mood. Whether it's a quick stretch, a dance break, or a short stroll, you'll discover how moving your body can unlock clarity for your mind.

The Science of Movement and Mental Clarity

Why does movement work so well? The answer lies in the remarkable connection between your body and brain. When you move, you're not just engaging your muscles—you're setting off a cascade of benefits that ripple through your entire system, from improved focus to elevated mood.

Boosting Blood Flow to the Brain

Movement increases circulation, delivering fresh oxygen and nutrients to your brain. Think of your mind as a thirsty plant: just as water revives wilting leaves, this rush of oxygen-rich blood energizes your brain, sharpening focus and enhancing cognitive function.

This is why even a quick stretch or a short walk can make you feel instantly more alert. It's like flipping on a mental light switch, illuminating ideas and solutions that felt out of reach just moments before.

Take Mateo, a graphic designer who often felt stuck in creative ruts. Whenever he hit a wall, he'd take a five-minute walk around his studio. By the time he returned, his thoughts felt clearer, and new ideas flowed effortlessly.

Endorphins: Your Brain's Mood Boosters

Physical activity releases endorphins, the body's natural "feel-good" chemicals. These neurotransmitters reduce stress, lift your mood, and create a sense of well-being that lingers long after you've finished moving.

Think of endorphins as your brain's way of rewarding you for taking care of yourself. Even low-intensity movement, like gentle stretches or a slow-paced walk, can trigger this chemical boost, leaving you feeling calmer and more positive.

For instance, Mia, a teacher, started incorporating light stretching into her lunch breaks. She was amazed at how much more patient and cheerful she felt in the afternoons, simply from giving her body a chance to reset.

Cognitive Supercharging

Movement also stimulates the production of brain-derived neurotrophic factor (BDNF), a protein that supports the growth of new neurons and strengthens existing connections in your brain. This means that regular movement doesn't just make you feel better in the moment—it actually enhances your brain's ability to learn, adapt, and problem-solve over time.

Imagine Sam, a software engineer preparing for a complex coding project. Before diving in, he spent five minutes doing jumping jacks and pacing his office. The burst of activity woke up his mind, helping him approach the project with sharper focus and a fresh perspective.

Counteracting Mental Fatigue

When you sit still for too long, your body starts to signal "rest mode," making it harder to concentrate. Movement breaks interrupt this pattern, re-energizing both your body and your mind.

Think of your brain as a muscle—it performs best when given regular periods of activity and recovery. Just as you wouldn't run a marathon without taking water breaks, you shouldn't expect your mind to stay sharp without occasional resets.

Consider Priya, a medical student who faced long hours of studying. She found that doing 10 squats or a short yoga flow every hour helped her stay focused and prevented the mental fog that used to creep in during marathon study sessions.

Reducing Cortisol and Stress

Stress activates your body's fight-or-flight response, flooding your system with cortisol, the stress hormone. While this response is helpful in true emergencies, prolonged stress can leave you feeling tense, anxious, and mentally scattered.

Movement offers an antidote. By engaging your body, you activate the parasympathetic nervous system—the "rest and digest" mode—which helps lower cortisol levels and restore balance.

Imagine Rachel, a marketing executive dealing with tight deadlines and high-stakes meetings. Whenever she felt her stress levels rising, she'd step outside for a brisk walk around the block. The simple act of moving her body helped her return to her desk feeling more grounded and capable.

A Mind-Body Connection That Works for You

The science is clear: movement isn't just good for your body—it's a lifeline for your mind. Whether it's boosting blood flow, releasing mood-enhancing endorphins, or building long-term brain health, the benefits of movement go far beyond physical fitness.

In the next sections, we'll dive into specific movement breaks that you can integrate seamlessly into your day. From desk-friendly stretches to energizing walks, you'll learn how to use movement as a powerful tool for mental clarity and emotional balance.

Quick Movement Breaks

No time for a full workout? No problem.

Here are five simple exercises you can do in five minutes or less:

1. Neck Rolls

- Drop your chin to your chest.

- Slowly roll your head to the right, back, left, and forward.

- Repeat a few times to release tension in your neck and shoulders.

2. Shoulder Shrugs

- Lift your shoulders up to your ears, hold for a second, then let them drop.

- Do this ten times to shake off built-up tension.

3. Seated Torso Twists

- Sit upright, place your right hand on the back of your chair, and twist your torso to the right.

- Hold for a few breaths, then switch sides.

4. Wrist and Finger Stretches

- Extend one arm, palm up, and gently pull back on your fingers with your other hand.

- Switch sides to stretch both wrists. Your hands will thank you, especially after hours at a keyboard.

5. Standing Calf Raises

- Stand up and lift your heels off the ground, then lower them back down.

- Repeat a few times to wake up your legs and get your blood flowing.

These exercises are quick, simple, and discreet enough to do almost anywhere—from your office to your living room. The next time you feel stuck, try one of these to refresh your body and mind.

Integrating Movement into Your Day

Movement breaks are most effective when they're consistent.

Here's how to make them a natural part of your routine:

1. Set a Timer

Use your phone or computer to remind you to move every hour. When the timer goes off, take a five-minute stretch or stand up and walk around.

2. Stand Up During Calls

If you're on a virtual meeting or phone call, stand up or pace around while you talk. You'll feel more engaged, and it's a simple way to stay active.

3. Take the Stairs

Whenever possible, skip the elevator. Climbing stairs is a quick, effective way to get your heart pumping.

4. Walk and Talk

Suggest a walking meeting for casual or brainstorming discussions. A change of scenery and fresh air can spark creativity and improve focus.

5. Pair Movement with Music

Create a playlist of your favorite upbeat songs. Use your break to stretch, dance, or simply move to the beat. It's like a mini dance party for one!

Why Movement Boosts Productivity

You might think stepping away from your desk wastes time, but the opposite is true.

Movement increases productivity by:

- **Sharpening Focus**: Physical activity delivers oxygen to the brain, clearing mental fog and improving concentration.

- **Enhancing Creativity**: The rhythmic motion of walking or stretching helps free your mind from rigid thought patterns, allowing new ideas to flow.

- **Reducing Errors**: Regular breaks reduce mental fatigue, leading to fewer mistakes and a more efficient workday.

Reflect and Apply

- **Reflect**: How does your energy level or focus feel right now?

- **Apply:** Pick one movement technique and try it today. How does it impact your mood or clarity?

- **Plan:** Commit to incorporating one movement break into your routine daily for the next week. Track your results.

Takeaway

Movement is a simple yet powerful way to refresh your mind and energize your body. Whether it's a five-minute walk, gentle stretches, or a moment of intentional movement during a busy day, these practices offer a quick reset for mental clarity and focus.

Choose one movement break that fits into your day, like standing stretches or a short outdoor walk. Notice how even a few minutes of movement shifts your mindset and boosts your energy.

While movement offers a powerful reset for your body and mind, sometimes all you need is one mindful minute. In the next chapter, we'll explore how this quick, intentional practice can create space for calm, clarity, and focus in the middle of even the busiest days.

Chapter Ten

The Mindful Minute: A Reset Ritual

How often do you find yourself rushing from one task to the next, your mind tangled in deadlines, notifications, and an endless stream of to-dos? Modern life has a way of pulling us into overdrive, leaving little room to pause, breathe, or simply be. But what if one minute—just sixty seconds—could create the space you need to reset, refocus, and recharge?

The Mindful Minute is exactly that: a simple yet powerful practice that helps you step out of the chaos and into the present moment. Think of it as hitting the pause button on your day—not to stop everything, but to slow it down just enough to regain clarity and calm.

Picture this: you're in the middle of a hectic workday, your shoulders tense and your thoughts racing. You pause, set a timer for one minute, close your eyes, and take a deep breath. For those sixty seconds, you focus on nothing but your breath, the sensations in your body, or the sounds around you. When the timer goes off, the tension in your chest has softened, and your mind feels lighter, like clearing a fogged mirror.

In a world that often feels too fast to keep up with, the Mindful Minute reminds us that a moment of stillness is always within reach. You don't need special equipment, a perfect environment, or even much time—just a willingness to pause, notice, and reset.

Why the Mindful Minute Works

The power of the Mindful Minute lies in its simplicity. While it may seem small, this single intentional pause can create a ripple effect, calming your nervous system, sharpening your focus, and transforming how you approach the rest of your day.

Breaking the Stress Cycle

When stress takes over, your body reacts automatically: your heart races, your breath becomes shallow, and your thoughts scatter. This is your fight-or-flight response kicking in—a survival mechanism designed to help you escape immediate danger. But in today's world, where the "dangers" are often emails, deadlines, and traffic jams, this response can leave you stuck in a cycle of tension and overwhelm.

The Mindful Minute interrupts that cycle. By pausing and focusing on your breath or senses, you activate your parasympathetic nervous system—the part of your body responsible for rest and recovery. This simple shift helps lower your heart rate, calm your mind, and bring you back to a state of balance.

For example, Sara, a busy parent juggling work and family, found herself constantly frazzled by the demands of her day. When she started taking a Mindful Minute before picking her kids up from school, she noticed a huge difference. The pause helped her transition from work mode to family mode, making her feel more present and patient with her children.

Grounding Yourself in the Present Moment

The human mind has a tendency to wander—to ruminate on the past or worry about the future. While this can be helpful for planning or learning, it often pulls us away from the here and now, creating a sense of disconnection and unease.

The Mindful Minute brings your attention back to the present moment, grounding you in what's real and tangible. Whether it's the sensation of your feet on the floor, the rhythm of your breath, or the sound of birds outside your window, this practice shifts your focus from "what if" to "what is."

Imagine Alex, an entrepreneur whose mind was always racing with ideas and responsibilities. During a particularly hectic week, he started using the Mindful Minute to reconnect with his surroundings. Each time he paused, he'd look out the window and notice the way the light shifted through the trees. These tiny moments of presence helped him feel calmer and more focused, even in the midst of chaos.

Maximizing Minimal Time

One of the most powerful aspects of the Mindful Minute is its accessibility. While other mindfulness practices may require more time, the Mindful Minute fits seamlessly into even the busiest schedules. It's short enough to feel doable but meaningful enough to make an impact.

Think of it like a sip of water when you're thirsty. It doesn't take long, but it refreshes you instantly. Over time, these one-minute resets add up, creating a foundation of mindfulness that supports you throughout your day.

Priya, a nurse working long, demanding shifts, found the Mindful Minute to be a lifesaver. Between seeing patients, she'd step into a quiet corner and spend sixty seconds focusing on her breath. Those brief pauses didn't just help her stay calm—they gave her the clarity to provide even better care.

Building Awareness and Intention

The Mindful Minute isn't just a tool for stress relief—it's a practice of awareness and intention. By taking a moment to pause and tune in, you're training your brain to notice your thoughts, feelings, and surroundings more clearly. This heightened awareness helps you respond to life with greater intention, rather than reacting on autopilot.

For instance, Javier, a marketing professional, realized that he often snapped at colleagues when he was feeling overwhelmed. After incorporating the Mindful Minute into his routine, he began noticing the signs of tension building up—clenched fists, a tight jaw, and racing thoughts. With this awareness, he could pause, take a Mindful Minute, and respond to challenges more calmly and constructively.

Your Reset, One Minute at a Time

The beauty of the Mindful Minute is its simplicity and versatility. Whether you're in the middle of a chaotic day or simply need a quick mental refresh, this practice offers a way to reconnect with yourself and the present moment.

In the next sections, we'll explore how to use the Mindful Minute in various situations, from managing stress to boosting focus. You'll discover practical techniques that fit seamlessly into your day, proving that even a single minute of mindfulness can create a powerful ripple effect in your life.

Mindful Minute Techniques

1. Breathing Awareness

Purpose: Use your breath to ground yourself and calm your thoughts.

Steps:

1. Sit or stand in a comfortable position.

2. Inhale deeply through your nose for a count of four.

3. Hold your breath for a count of four.

4. Exhale slowly through your mouth for a count of six.

5. Repeat the cycle for 60 seconds, focusing on the rhythm of your breath.

Why It Works: Intentional breathing lowers your heart rate and activates your relaxation response, helping you regain a sense of control.

Real-Life Example: Before presenting her quarterly report, Amanda felt a wave of anxiety. She stepped into a quiet corner and practiced Breathing Awareness for one minute. By the time she walked into the room, her nerves had settled, and she felt more confident.

2. Sensory Scan

Purpose: Use your senses to anchor yourself in the present moment.

Steps:

1. Take a slow, deep breath and look around.

2. Identify one thing you can see, one thing you can hear, and one

thing you can feel.

3. Spend a few seconds noticing the details: the colors, textures, or patterns of what you see; the volume and rhythm of what you hear; the temperature or texture of what you feel.

4. Repeat the process with new sensory inputs until the minute is up.

Why It Works: Shifting your focus outward interrupts overthinking and grounds you in the now, providing a quick mental reset.

Real-Life Example: During a heated team discussion, Jack felt frustration bubbling up. He used the Sensory Scan technique to notice the hum of the air conditioner, the grain of wood on the conference table, and the coolness of his chair. This simple shift helped him regain composure and contribute more thoughtfully to the conversation.

3. Gratitude Snapshot

Purpose: Shift your perspective by focusing on what you're grateful for.

Steps:

1. Close your eyes and take a deep breath.

2. Think of one thing that brought you joy or comfort recently. It could be something as simple as a kind word from a friend, a warm cup of tea, or the sound of rain.

3. Picture the moment in detail—where were you, what did it look or feel like, and why did it make you smile?

4. Breathe in gratitude for that moment, letting the positive feelings fill you.

Why It Works: Gratitude reorients your mind toward positivity, helping you approach the next moment with more optimism and calm.

Real-Life Example: Stuck in traffic, Mia practiced the Gratitude Snapshot. She pictured her toddler's laughter from that morning and felt the tension in her shoulders ease.

4. Visualization Reset

Purpose: Create a mental image that replaces stress with calm.

Steps:

1. Close your eyes and take a slow, deep breath.

2. Imagine a peaceful scene that makes you feel safe and relaxed—a forest, a beach, or a cozy nook.

3. Picture the details: the colors, sounds, and sensations of the scene.

4. Spend the next 60 seconds immersed in this mental retreat.

Why It Works: Visualization provides a mental escape from stress, re-setting your emotional state in just a minute.

Real-Life Example: Overwhelmed by her inbox, Clara practiced the Visualization Reset. Imagining herself walking through a sunlit meadow helped her return to her desk with a clearer mind.

How to Make the Mindful Minute a Habit

- **Set Triggers**: Link your Mindful Minute to daily activities, like waiting in line, before meals, or after meetings.

- **Use Prompts**: Keep a sticky note on your desk or set a phone reminder labeled "Take a Minute."

- **Track Your Practice**: Reflect on when and how you use the Mindful Minute, noting the impact on your mood and focus.

Reflect and Apply

Reflect: What part of your day feels most chaotic or overwhelming? How could a Mindful Minute help?

Apply: Try practicing one technique today. How does it make you feel afterward?

Plan: Commit to a 7-day Mindful Minute challenge, incorporating one practice each day. Notice how it changes your mindset or stress levels.

Takeaway

The Mindful Minute is proof that meaningful change doesn't have to take hours. In just 60 seconds, you can reset your mind, ground your emotions, and approach life with greater clarity and calm. It's a small investment with powerful returns.

As the Mindful Minute helps you reset internally, connecting with nature can extend this sense of calm and clarity. In the next chapter, we'll explore how nature's beauty and stillness can profoundly impact your well-being, even in small doses.

Chapter Eleven

Nature's Impact on Your Well-Being

Close your eyes for a moment and picture yourself standing in a forest. The air is crisp and cool, carrying the faint scent of pine and earth. A gentle breeze stirs the leaves above, creating a soothing rustle that mixes with the distant chirp of birds. Under your feet, the ground feels solid, grounding you, as sunlight filters through the canopy in golden streams. In this moment, something shifts. Your shoulders relax, your breath deepens, and the weight of the world seems to ease just a little.

This is the quiet magic of nature—a power so subtle yet profound that it can transform not only your mood but your overall well-being.

In our modern lives, surrounded by screens and schedules, nature often feels like a distant luxury, something reserved for vacations or rare free weekends. But science and experience tell us otherwise. Even small doses of time outdoors—a walk in the park, sitting under a tree, or tending to a garden—can have measurable benefits for your mind and body.

Nature doesn't just soothe; it heals. It reduces stress, sharpens focus, boosts creativity, and even strengthens your immune system. It connects you to something larger than yourself, reminding you of your place in a vast and intricate world.

This chapter isn't about urging you to escape to a remote mountain cabin or spend hours hiking rugged trails. It's about rediscovering the pockets of nature that already exist in your daily life and learning how to embrace them as a resource for balance, clarity, and well-being. Whether it's the view from your window, the feel of grass under your feet, or the sound of rain against the pavement, nature is always there—ready to restore and replenish you, one moment at a time.

Why Nature Heals

The Biophilia Effect

Humans have an innate connection to nature, a concept known as **biophilia**. For thousands of years, we thrived in natural environments, relying on them for survival. Modern urban life may separate us from the outdoors, but our brains and bodies still respond to nature with feelings of calm and safety.

Research supports this connection. Studies show that spending time in green spaces activates brain regions linked to emotional regulation and reduces activity in the prefrontal cortex—where stress and rumination often reside. Simply put, nature provides a mental reprieve.

Stress Relief at Its Best

When you're surrounded by nature, your body's stress response starts to unwind. The sounds of leaves rustling or waves lapping at the shore engage your **parasympathetic nervous system**, signaling your body that it's time to relax.

Even urban greenery can make a difference. Studies reveal that gazing at trees or even pictures of natural landscapes reduce cortisol, the hormone linked to stress, and lowers heart rate and blood pressure.

Sharper Focus and Mental Clarity

Nature serves as a reset button for your brain. When we're overstimulated by screens, deadlines, and multitasking, our mental energy gets depleted—a phenomenon known as **directed attention fatigue**. Nature provides effortless attention, allowing the brain to recover.

This principle is explained by the **Attention Restoration Theory**, which suggests that natural environments restore our capacity for focus, memory, and creativity. Whether it's brainstorming solutions on a walk or simply feeling more present after time outdoors, nature recharges the mind.

Physical and Emotional Well-Being

Nature doesn't just calm the mind—it strengthens the body. Sunlight boosts serotonin levels, improving mood and promoting better sleep. Exposure to nature has even been linked to improved immune function, thanks to phytoncides—natural compounds released by trees.

In Japan, the practice of **forest bathing** (spending mindful time in wooded areas) has become a cornerstone of preventative health care. Research shows it reduces symptoms of depression and anxiety, improves cardiovascular health, and fosters a profound sense of well-being.

Nature Practices for Everyday Life

1. The 5-Minute Nature Walk

Take a quick stroll, focusing on your surroundings. Notice the colors of the leaves, the sound of birds, or the warmth of sunlight on your skin.

Variation:

- In an urban area, focus on the architectural patterns of trees lining streets or small pockets of greenery.

- In rural settings, observe the horizon, the movement of water, or the sounds of animals.

2. Grounding with Barefoot Walks

Kick off your shoes and walk on grass, sand, or soil. Feel the texture beneath your feet and imagine the Earth's energy grounding and recharging you.

Why It Works: Grounding reduces inflammation, improves sleep, and fosters a deep sense of connection with nature.

3. Forest Bathing Mini-Guide

Find a wooded area, whether it's a park or a trail. Spend 5 minutes walking slowly, pausing to notice details like the patterns on bark, the smell of pine, or the play of light through leaves.

Tip: You don't need to "do" anything—simply observe and enjoy the stillness.

4. Indoor Nature Immersion

Can't step outside? Bring nature to you:

- Add plants to your desk or living space.

- Use a nature-inspired playlist with waves, rain, or birdsong.

- Place photos or art featuring natural landscapes in your work-space.

Why It Works: Even visual or auditory cues from nature can activate the brain's relaxation response.

Case Study: Finding Calm in Nature

After a particularly stressful week juggling work and family demands, Johanna felt completely drained. Her therapist suggested she try forest bathing. Skeptical at first, she drove to a nearby trail and spent several minutes walking slowly, noticing the sounds of birds and the texture of the forest floor beneath her feet.

By the end of her walk, she felt lighter. She repeated the practice weekly, finding it became her go-to strategy for stress relief. Over time, the moments of calm she experienced in the forest began to spill over into her daily life.

The 7-Day Nature Reset Challenge

If you're new to integrating nature into your routine, this challenge will help you get started:

- **Day 1**: Take a 5-minute walk and notice three things you've never observed before.

- **Day 2**: Spend 10 minutes outdoors without your phone. Focus on your breathing.

- **Day 3**: Add a plant to your space or sit near a window with natural light.

- **Day 4**: Try grounding—stand barefoot on grass or sand for a few minutes.

- **Day 5**: Listen to a nature playlist while working or relaxing.

- **Day 6**: Write about a time nature helped you feel calm or joyful.

- **Day 7**: Take a mindful nature walk, engaging all your senses.

At the end of the week, reflect on how your relationship with nature has shifted.

Reflect and Apply

- **Reflect**: How do you currently interact with nature? Are there opportunities to integrate it more into your routine?

- **Apply**: Try one practice today and note how it affects your mood or clarity.

- **Plan**: Commit to a specific nature ritual, such as a weekly walk or adding more greenery to your home.

Takeaway

Nature isn't just a backdrop; it's a source of renewal and connection. Whether it's a walk in the park, grounding your feet on the earth, or simply observing a tree outside your window, spending time with nature can calm your mind, reduce stress, and foster a sense of balance.

Explore how you can incorporate nature into your day, even in small ways. Take a moment to step outside, feel the sunlight on your skin, or listen to the rustle of leaves.

While nature connects you to the world around you, journaling offers a chance to connect deeply with yourself. In the next chapter, we'll dive into how putting pen to paper can help you clarify your thoughts, process emotions, and uncover new insights.

Chapter Twelve

Mindful Eating in 5 Minutes

Let's talk about eating—something we all do, but rarely give much thought to. We rush through breakfast, multitask during lunch, and scarf down dinner while binge-watching our favorite shows. But what if we slowed down? What if we really *noticed* our food?

Mindful eating transforms mealtime from a routine habit into a sensory experience. It's like watching a black-and-white movie suddenly shift into vibrant color. When you're mindful, every bite becomes a celebration of flavor, texture, and nourishment. Let's explore how mindful eating can boost your digestion, elevate your meals, and bring a sense of calm into your day—all in just five minutes.

What Is Mindful Eating?

Mindful eating is the practice of fully focusing on your food and the experience of eating. It's not about dieting, calorie counting, or sticking to a specific food plan—it's about bringing your full attention to the act of nourishing your body.

Think of mindful eating as a way to strengthen your connection with food. Instead of rushing through meals or multitasking, you slow down, engage your senses, and savor every bite. It's like taking a high-definition snapshot of your meal—tasting every flavor, noticing every texture, and appreciating the effort that brought the food to your plate.

But mindful eating goes beyond just tasting your food. It's also about listening to your body. Are you hungry, or are you eating out of boredom? Are you satisfied, or are you pushing past fullness? Mindful eating helps you tune into these cues so you can make more intentional choices.

Why Mindful Eating Matters

In today's fast-paced world, eating often becomes a secondary activity. We grab breakfast on the go, eat lunch in front of our screens, and rush through dinner while scrolling through our phones. This mindless approach to eating disconnects us from the food we're consuming and can lead to overeating, poor digestion, and reduced satisfaction.

Mindful eating flips the script. By focusing on your meal, you give your body the chance to truly enjoy and benefit from the nourishment you're providing. Studies show that mindful eating can improve digestion, enhance satisfaction, and even reduce emotional eating by helping you identify and respond to hunger cues more effectively.

For example, imagine you're eating a bowl of soup while answering emails. Chances are, you'll finish the soup without even realizing how it tasted. But if you pause, take a deep breath, and focus on the warmth, aroma, and flavors of the soup, the experience becomes richer and more satisfying.

The Science Behind Mindful Eating

Mindful eating isn't just a feel-good practice—it's backed by science.

Here's what happens when you slow down and focus on your meal:

- **Improved Digestion**: Chewing slowly and eating at a relaxed pace gives your digestive system time to process food efficiently. This can reduce bloating and discomfort.

- **Enhanced Brain Signals**: When you eat mindfully, your brain has time to register feelings of fullness. This helps prevent overeating and allows you to stop when you're satisfied.

- **Reduced Stress**: Focusing on your meal pulls you out of the rush of daily life, creating a moment of calm. This reduces stress hormones like cortisol, making meals a more restorative experience.

- **Increased Enjoyment**: When you savor your food, you engage your senses more deeply, making each bite more satisfying. This often leads to greater overall happiness with your meals.

Mindful Eating as Self-Care

At its core, mindful eating is a form of self-care. It's a way of honoring your body's needs and creating a moment of calm in your day. In a world where we're constantly rushing from one thing to the next, pausing to truly enjoy a meal can feel revolutionary.

You don't have to be perfect to practice mindful eating. Perhaps start with one meal or snack a day—and build from there. Whether it's a home-cooked dinner or a quick snack, every opportunity to eat is a chance to practice mindfulness and reconnect with yourself.

Five Simple Practices for Mindful Eating

Ready to try mindful eating?

Here are five easy ways to get started:

1. Put Your Phone Down: This one's a game-changer. When you scroll through social media or answer emails during meals, you're distracted from the experience. Put your phone aside and give your meal your full attention. It's like a little gift to yourself—a moment to pause and focus on what's in front of you.

2. Engage Your Senses: Before taking a bite, pause and observe your food. Notice the colors, shapes, and textures. Smell the aroma. When you finally taste it, focus on the flavors. Is it sweet, salty, or savory? How do the textures feel in your mouth? Engaging your senses creates a deeper appreciation for what you're eating.

3. Chew Slowly: Chewing isn't just for politeness—it's a key part of digestion. Aim to chew each bite at least 20 times. This slows you down and gives your body time to process the food. You'll also discover subtle flavors and textures you might have missed.

4. Pause Between Bites: After swallowing, take a moment to breathe. Check in with your body. Are you still hungry? Are you starting to feel satisfied? Pausing helps you tune into your body's natural signals, preventing overeating and enhancing your enjoyment.

5. Express Gratitude: Before or during your meal, take a moment to appreciate where your food came from. Whether it's a home-cooked dish or takeout, acknowledge the effort it took to bring that meal to your plate. Gratitude deepens your connection to your food and makes each bite more meaningful.

Savoring Your Food

Mindful eating isn't just about slowing down—it's about savoring every bite.

Here's how to make your meals feel like a special occasion, even on an ordinary day:

- **Mindful Bites**: Take smaller bites and let the flavors linger on your tongue. Think of it like sipping a fine wine instead of gulping it down.

- **Focus on Texture**: Notice the crunchiness of a salad, the creaminess of mashed potatoes, or the chewiness of bread. Engaging with texture keeps you present and makes meals more enjoyable.

- **Pay Attention to Temperature**: Hot soups, cool salads, and warm bread—temperature plays a big role in how we experience food. Notice how it enhances the flavors and sensations of your meal.

- **Reflect on Emotions**: Food often carries memories and emotions. Does this meal remind you of a family gathering or a special trip? Reflecting on these connections can bring even more joy to your dining experience.

Overcoming the "I'm Too Busy" Mentality

Life is busy, and it can feel impossible to carve out time for mindfulness. But mindful eating doesn't have to take an hour—it can be done in just five minutes.

Here's How to Start:

- **Set a Timer**: Before eating, take one minute to center yourself. Breathe deeply, set an intention for your meal, and prepare to enjoy every bite.

- **Choose One Practice**: You don't have to do it all. Pick one mindful eating exercise—like pausing between bites—and focus on that.

- **Reflect Afterward**: When you finish your meal, take a moment to reflect. Did you enjoy the experience? Did you notice anything new about your food?

Even small efforts can make a big difference. It's not about perfection—it's about bringing a little more presence into your day.

The Benefits of Mindful Eating

Mindful eating isn't just about enjoying your meals—it's a practice that positively impacts your body, mind, and overall relationship with food. By slowing down and paying attention, you unlock a host of benefits that go beyond the plate. Let's dive into the key advantages of mindful eating and how they can transform your mealtimes.

1. Better Digestion: When you eat mindfully, you give your body the time it needs to properly process food. Chewing slowly and thoroughly breaks down food more effectively, making it easier for your digestive system to do its job. This can reduce bloating, indigestion, and discomfort after meals.

Think about it: when you rush through a meal, your stomach is left to handle food that hasn't been adequately broken down. By chewing each bite thoroughly, you're helping your body absorb nutrients more efficiently. It's a simple change that makes a big difference.

2. Enhanced Satisfaction: Have you ever finished a meal and felt like you barely tasted it? That's what happens when we eat on autopilot. Mindful eating changes this by encouraging you to savor every bite. When you engage your senses—tasting, smelling, and feeling the textures of your food—you naturally enjoy it more.

This satisfaction isn't just about flavors; it's about the experience. Whether it's a perfectly ripe strawberry or a hearty bowl of soup, mindful eating turns ordinary meals into moments of appreciation.

3. Better Portion Control: Mindful eating helps you tune into your body's hunger and fullness cues, making it easier to stop eating when you're satisfied—not stuffed. When you eat quickly or while distracted, it's easy to overshoot and eat more than your body needs.

By pausing between bites and checking in with yourself, you create space to recognize when you've had enough. Over time, this practice can help you maintain a healthy relationship with food and avoid overeating.

4. Reduced Emotional Eating: For many of us, food isn't just fuel—it's comfort. Stress, boredom, or sadness can lead to emotional eating, where we turn to food to cope with feelings. While it's perfectly normal to find joy in food, relying on it as a sole source of comfort can create an unhealthy cycle.

Mindful eating helps you recognize the difference between physical hunger and emotional hunger. By paying attention to your body's signals, you can make more intentional choices about when and why you eat. This awareness creates space for healthier coping mechanisms, like journaling, taking a walk, or talking to a friend.

5. Improved Focus and Reduced Stress: Mealtimes can become moments of calm in an otherwise hectic day. When you eat mindfully, you're fully present with your food, pulling your focus away from work, screens, or stressors. This break from multitasking helps lower cortisol levels—the hormone associated with stress—and leaves you feeling more centered.

Incorporating mindfulness into meals also has a ripple effect. It trains your brain to focus on the present moment, a skill that carries over into other areas of life, like work or relationships.

6. A Healthier Relationship with Food: Mindful eating helps shift your mindset from seeing food as a source of guilt or anxiety to viewing it as nourishment and joy. It's not about rigid rules or deprivation—it's about celebrating the experience of eating and honoring your body's needs.

For example, instead of labeling foods as "good" or "bad," mindful eating encourages you to explore how different foods make you feel. Does that sugary snack give you energy or leave you feeling sluggish? Does a balanced meal keep you satisfied or leave you craving more? These insights empower you to make choices that truly serve you.

7. Greater Appreciation and Gratitude: When you eat mindfully, you naturally develop a deeper appreciation for your food. From the farmers who grew the ingredients to the person who prepared the meal (even if that's you!), there's a lot to be thankful for.

Taking a moment to express gratitude before eating—whether it's a simple "thank you" or a silent acknowledgment—can make meals more meaningful. This practice also cultivates a positive mindset, reminding you of the abundance in your life.

Real-Life Impacts

Here's how mindful eating can play out in everyday life:

- **At Work**: Instead of eating lunch at your desk while answering emails, step away for a few minutes. Focus on your food, and notice how much more energized and productive you feel afterward.

- **With Family**: Practice mindful eating during family meals by putting phones away and engaging in conversation. It turns mealtime into a bonding experience instead of a rushed routine.

- **On the Go**: Even when eating in a hurry, you can pause to take a deep breath, notice the flavors of your food, and express gratitude. It's not about perfection—it's about small, intentional moments.

A Lasting Impact

The benefits of mindful eating extend far beyond the meal itself. By fostering awareness and intention around food, you create a ripple effect that improves your overall well-being. You'll feel more in tune with your body, more present in your daily life, and more connected to the nourishment that sustains you.

Mindful eating isn't a chore—it's a gift you give yourself. With each bite, you're not just feeding your body—you're nurturing your mind and spirit.

Take the Mindful Eating Challenge

Ready to give it a try? Here's a quick challenge: For your next meal, pick one mindful eating practice and commit to it. Whether it's chewing slowly, engaging your senses, or expressing gratitude, notice how it changes your experience.

Over time, these small moments of mindfulness will add up, transforming how you approach food and mealtimes. You'll find yourself savoring flavors, appreciating textures, and feeling more connected to your meals—and to yourself.

Remember, mindfulness isn't about being perfect. If you slip up or eat in a rush, it's okay. Just take a deep breath and try again. Each meal is an opportunity to practice and grow.

Now, grab your fork, take a deep breath, and enjoy that first mindful bite. Your taste buds—and your body—will thank you!

Takeaway

Mindful eating isn't just about the food on your plate—it's about how you consume and engage with the world around you. Just as paying attention to what and how you eat can foster a deeper connection to your body and emotions, the same principle applies to how you interact with technology.

In our hyperconnected world, it's easy to get lost in an endless stream of notifications, emails, and social media. Mindful tech use invites you to consume technology with intention, creating space for focus, calm, and balance. Let's explore how a digital detox can help you reset your relationship with technology.

Chapter Thirteen

Digital Detox: Mindfulness in Tech

Technology is woven into every part of our lives. It connects us, entertains us, and makes life more convenient. But let's be honest—there's a downside too. How many times have you found yourself mindlessly scrolling late into the night, only to wake up feeling anxious or exhausted? Or checking your phone during a conversation, realizing you missed half of what was said?

Tech is like a double-edged sword. On one side, it's a powerful tool for productivity and connection. On the other, it can trap us in an endless cycle of distraction, comparison, and overwhelm. It's no wonder so many of us feel mentally drained by our devices.

The problem isn't technology itself—it's how we use it. Without boundaries, tech can take over, dominating our time and attention. But with mindfulness, we can strike a balance that allows us to benefit from technology without losing ourselves in it.

This chapter is about reclaiming your relationship with tech. It's about learning how to use your devices intentionally, creating space for the things that truly matter, and building habits that support your mental well-being. Let's explore the impact of tech overload and the simple steps you can take to create a healthier, more balanced digital life.

The Impact of Tech Overload

Imagine this: You're adding apps to your phone—social media, news alerts, productivity tools—without deleting the old ones. Each app runs in the background, draining your battery and slowing your system. Eventually, your phone lags, freezes, or shuts down altogether.

Now, picture your brain as that phone. Every notification, email, and endless scroll takes up space in your mental bandwidth. When there's too much noise, your mind struggles to focus, process information, and recharge.

The Science of Overload

Studies show that excessive screen time isn't just tiring—it can have serious effects on mental health. Research from the American Psychological Association reveals that more than 60% of Americans feel overwhelmed by digital information. This constant barrage of content leads to:

- **Increased Stress Levels**: Notifications and alerts keep your brain in a state of hyper-vigilance, triggering a stress response that's hard to shut off.

- **Higher Rates of Anxiety and Depression**: Social media comparison, doomscrolling, and endless digital multitasking can contribute to feelings of inadequacy and overwhelm.

- **Reduced Attention Span**: With so much information competing for your focus, it becomes harder to concentrate on any one thing for long.

The Physical Toll

Tech overload doesn't just affect your mind—it impacts your body too. Staring at screens for long periods can cause digital eye strain, headaches, and even sleep disruptions due to blue light exposure. And let's not forget the toll of sitting hunched over devices, which can lead to neck, back, and wrist pain.

Social Disconnection

Ironically, the very tools designed to connect us can also isolate us. Instead of engaging in meaningful face-to-face interactions, we often find ourselves glued to our screens, scrolling through highlight reels and filtered photos. This digital connection often lacks the depth and fulfillment of real-life relationships.

A Growing Dependence

Our reliance on technology has only grown in recent years. Many of us start and end our days with our devices, checking emails before our feet hit the floor and scrolling social media until we drift off to sleep. While tech is undeniably useful, this constant availability can blur the boundaries between work, rest, and play.

Consider this: If you spend just two hours a day on social media, that's 730 hours a year. What could you do with that time if it weren't spent scrolling? The reality is, tech isn't going anywhere—but how we engage with it can make all the difference.

Quick Tips to Reduce Screen Time

Here are some easy ways to start unplugging and giving your brain a break:

1. Set Screen Time Limits: Use apps like "Moment" or "Screen Time" to track your usage. Seeing how much time you spend online can be a wake-up call. Once you know where your hours go, set realistic goals to cut back.

2. Create Tech-Free Zones: Designate areas in your home where screens aren't allowed. The dinner table and bedroom are great places to start. Eating without scrolling fosters connection, and a screen-free bedroom improves sleep.

3. Schedule Regular Breaks: Take a five-minute screen break every hour. Use this time to stretch, hydrate, or gaze out the window. Not only does this rest your eyes, but it also refreshes your mind.

4. Use "Do Not Disturb" Mode: Enable this feature during focused work hours or when you're winding down for bed. It silences unnecessary pings and helps you stay present.

5. Prioritize Offline Activities: Rediscover the joys of real life. Read a book, cook a meal, or go for a walk. These moments of unplugged connection remind you of the richness outside your screen.

Cultivating a Balanced Relationship with Tech

It's not about abandoning tech altogether—it's about making it work for you, not against you. Here's how to use tech more mindfully:

1. Practice Mindful Consumption: Before diving into your apps or social media feeds, pause and ask yourself: "Why am I logging on? What do I hope to gain?" Be selective about the content you consume. If something doesn't serve you—unfollow, mute, or delete.

2. Schedule Digital Detox Days: Pick one day a week to unplug completely. No phones, no laptops—just you and the world around you. It might feel strange at first, but it's incredibly refreshing to reconnect with yourself and your environment.

3. Engage with Purpose: When you're online, do so with intention. Whether you're connecting with friends, seeking inspiration, or learning something new, focus on making your screen time meaningful.

4. Reflect on Your Usage: At the end of the week, think about your relationship with tech. Did it leave you feeling energized or drained? This awareness helps you tweak your habits and find balance.

A Personal Story

I used to be glued to my phone. It was the first thing I checked in the morning and the last thing I saw before bed. My friends joked that I was practically fused to it. But one day, I realized how much I was missing—the little moments with family, the beauty of a sunset, or even just the calm of an evening without constant pings.

So, I made changes. I set screen time limits, created tech-free zones, and started taking digital detox days. It wasn't easy at first—I felt like I was missing out. But over time, I noticed how much more present and happy I felt. I still use tech daily, but now, it's on my terms.

Actionable Steps for Your Digital Detox

Ready to reclaim your mental clarity?

Start with these small, achievable steps:

1. **Track Your Screen Time:** Use an app or jot it down in a notebook. Awareness is the first step to change.

2. **Establish a Tech-Free Zone:** Choose one area of your home where screens are off-limits. Commit to keeping it screen-free for

a week and notice the difference.

3. **Schedule a Digital Detox Day:** Pick one day this week to go offline completely. Treat it like a self-care ritual—a chance to recharge and refocus.

4. **Reflect Weekly:** Every Sunday, think about how your tech usage affected your mood and productivity. Adjust your habits as needed.

5. **Involve Others:** Share your digital detox goals with a friend or family member. Accountability makes it easier to stay on track.

Why It Matters

Technology is a tool, not your master. By setting boundaries and using it mindfully, you can reduce stress, improve focus, and create space for the things that truly matter.

You don't have to be perfect. It's not about quitting tech cold turkey—it's about small, intentional changes that add up over time. So, take that first step today. Set a timer, create a tech-free zone, or simply pause before picking up your phone.

Your mind—and your life—will thank you.

Takeaway

Technology connects us to the world, but it can also overwhelm and distract us. A digital detox isn't about abandoning your devices—it's about using them intentionally to support your well-being. By setting boundaries and creating mindful tech habits, you can reclaim your focus, energy, and peace of mind.

Start today by identifying one small change you can make, like setting screen-free times or creating a mindful morning routine. Notice how these intentional breaks bring clarity and balance to your day.

While a digital detox brings silence and space, music can serve as a mindful tool to center and uplift you. In the next chapter, we'll explore how sound and rhythm can enhance your mindfulness practice and create moments of calm and joy.

Chapter Fourteen

The Role of Music in Mindfulness

Music has this uncanny ability to weave itself into every corner of our lives. It's there when you're celebrating, comforting you during tough times, or simply filling the silence on a long commute. From the nostalgic song that takes you back to your childhood to the beats that get you moving on a lazy morning, music isn't just background noise—it's a companion.

But what if music could be more than just a soundtrack to your day? What if it could become a tool for mindfulness, a way to soothe your mind and reset your focus in just a few minutes?

Think about the last time you listened to a piece of music that moved you. Maybe it was a soulful melody that brought tears to your eyes or an uplifting tune that had you tapping your feet. That emotional connection isn't just coincidence—it's a reflection of how deeply music affects our brains and bodies. Studies show that music can lower stress hormones, boost feel-good chemicals, and even help us find clarity in the middle of chaos.

In a world that's constantly noisy—filled with notifications, responsibilities, and mental clutter—music can become your refuge. It has the power to create a bubble of calm amidst the storm, to refocus your thoughts when they're scattered, and to guide you gently back to the present moment.

This chapter is all about harnessing that power. We'll explore the science of how music affects your brain, practical ways to use music and sound therapy in your mindfulness practice, and actionable steps to bring these techniques into your daily life. Whether you're a music enthusiast or someone who rarely presses play, you'll find simple, effective ways to use sound as a tool for relaxation and focus.

So, let's turn up the volume and dive into the transformative role of music in mindfulness.

Why Music Works as a Mindfulness Tool

Music has a unique ability to reach parts of our mind and soul that words often can't. It's not just a collection of sounds; it's an experience that interacts with our emotions, memory, and physiology. But why does music work so well as a mindfulness tool? Let's unpack its power to calm the mind, center your focus, and elevate your mood.

1. It Engages Your Brain's Chemistry

When you listen to music, your brain lights up like a switchboard. It releases dopamine, the chemical responsible for pleasure and motivation, and reduces cortisol, the hormone linked to stress. This dual action creates a sense of balance, making music both calming and uplifting.

For example, slow-tempo tracks with gentle melodies can lower your heart rate and blood pressure, helping your body shift from a state of stress to relaxation. Meanwhile, upbeat songs can energize and motivate, giving you that extra push when you're feeling drained.

Research has also shown that music stimulates the brain's reward system, which is why a favorite song can instantly make you feel good. This ability to influence brain chemistry makes music a powerful tool for managing emotions and cultivating mindfulness.

2. It Anchors You in the Present Moment

One of the hallmarks of mindfulness is staying present—fully experiencing the here and now. Music naturally facilitates this by engaging your senses. The rhythm grounds you, the melody captures your attention, and the harmony provides emotional resonance.

Think about it: when you focus on a song, you're less likely to ruminate on the past or worry about the future. Instead, you become immersed in the texture of the sound, the rise and fall of the notes, and the emotions it evokes. This act of deep listening is a mindfulness practice in itself, one that quiets mental chatter and brings you back to the present moment.

3. It Enhances Emotional Awareness

Music taps into our emotions like nothing else. A melancholic tune can help you process sadness, while an upbeat anthem might fill you with joy. This emotional resonance makes music a valuable tool for mindfulness, as it allows you to acknowledge and explore your feelings in a safe, structured way.

For instance, if you're feeling overwhelmed, playing a soothing piece of music can help you gently name and release those emotions. On the flip side, if you're feeling low-energy, a motivational playlist can boost your mood and reset your focus. By aligning with your emotional state, music becomes a companion in your mindfulness journey, helping you navigate and make sense of your inner world.

4. It Creates a Sense of Connection

Music has a way of making you feel connected—not just to yourself, but to others and the world around you. Whether it's a nostalgic song that reminds you of a loved one or a nature-inspired track that evokes the serenity of a forest, music bridges the gap between your inner and outer worlds.

This connection is vital for mindfulness. When you feel linked to something greater than yourself, it becomes easier to let go of stress, embrace the present, and find a sense of peace.

5. It's Accessible Anytime, Anywhere

Unlike many mindfulness practices that require a specific time or setting, music is always within reach. Whether you're commuting, cooking dinner, or taking a break at work, you can turn on a song and instantly create a moment of calm.

Even better, music doesn't demand your full attention to be effective. While deep listening enhances mindfulness, even having calming tunes playing in the background can reduce stress and improve focus. This flexibility makes it one of the most accessible mindfulness tools available.

6. It Fosters Creativity and Focus

Have you ever noticed how the right music can get you "in the zone"? Instrumental tracks or ambient sounds, in particular, are great for fostering concentration. They drown out distractions, create a steady rhythm for your mind to follow, and make repetitive tasks feel more engaging.

This connection between music and creativity isn't just anecdotal—it's backed by science. Studies show that music activates the brain's prefrontal cortex, which is responsible for decision-making, problem-solving, and focus. When used mindfully, music can help you enter a state of flow, where you're fully absorbed in the task at hand.

The Science of Sound and the Mind

The therapeutic effects of music are so profound that they've become a field of study in their own right. Music therapy, for example, is used to treat conditions ranging from anxiety and depression to chronic pain and trauma. This isn't just about listening to your favorite tunes—it's about the intentional use of sound to support mental and emotional health.

From classical compositions to binaural beats, the key lies in matching the music to your needs. Slower tempos for relaxation, rhythmic beats for focus, or nature sounds for grounding—there's a perfect track for every state of mind.

Music is more than entertainment; it's a powerful mindfulness tool that engages your brain, soothes your emotions, and anchors you in the present. Whether you're creating a calming playlist, experimenting with sound therapy, or simply letting a favorite song wash over you, music offers an accessible and enjoyable way to cultivate mindfulness in your daily life.

So, next time you press play, take a moment to truly listen. Feel the rhythm, notice the melody, and let the music guide you toward a state of balance and clarity.

Creating a 5-Minute Playlist for Instant Calm

Sometimes, all you need is five minutes of the right music to reset your mood and bring you back to center.

Here's how to craft your own calming playlist:

1. Choose Your Vibe: Start by asking yourself what kind of sound soothes you. Is it the gentle strum of an acoustic guitar? The elegance of classical piano? Maybe ambient nature sounds or soft vocals? There's no right or wrong—it's about what resonates with you.

2. Select Your Tracks: Pick three to five songs that bring you peace. If you're stuck, try exploring playlists labeled "Relaxing," "Chill," or "Mindfulness" on your favorite streaming service. A few go-to genres include:

- Ambient or instrumental music

- Classical pieces by composers like Debussy or Satie

- Soft acoustic tracks

- Nature-inspired sounds like rain or ocean waves

3. Keep It Short and Sweet: The goal is to create a quick escape, not a full concert. Limit your playlist to around five minutes so it feels manageable, even on your busiest days.

4. Make It Accessible: Save your playlist somewhere easy to reach—on your phone, computer, or even a smart speaker. When stress strikes, you'll be able to press play without fumbling.

5. Hit Play and Breathe: Find a quiet spot, close your eyes, and let the music envelop you. Pair it with deep breathing for an even greater sense of calm. Feel the tension in your body release as the sounds carry you to a peaceful mental space.

Exploring Sound Therapy

Sound therapy is an ancient practice that uses the power of sound to calm the mind, restore balance, and promote emotional well-being. From the resonant tones of singing bowls to the rhythmic beat of drums, sound has been used for centuries as a tool for healing and mindfulness.

Modern sound therapy builds on these traditions, using scientifically designed techniques to reduce stress, improve focus, and enhance relaxation. Let's explore some of the most popular sound therapy methods and how they can become part of your mindfulness journey.

1. Binaural Beats

Binaural beats are a type of auditory illusion created when you listen to two slightly different frequencies in each ear. Your brain perceives a third frequency—known as the binaural beat—that can influence your mental state.

- **How It Works**: Binaural beats are thought to stimulate brainwave activity, helping your mind shift into specific states like relaxation, focus, or creativity. For example, alpha waves (8–14 Hz) are associated with calmness and meditation, while beta waves (14–30 Hz) promote alertness and focus.

- **How to Use It**: All you need is a pair of headphones and a quiet space. Search for binaural beat tracks online, choose one that aligns with your goals (e.g., relaxation, focus, or sleep), and listen for at least 5–10 minutes. It's a great way to reset your mind during a busy day or unwind before bed.

2. Nature Sounds

There's something inherently calming about the sounds of nature. Whether it's the gentle patter of rain, the rustle of leaves, or the rhythmic crash of ocean waves, these sounds tap into our primal connection with the natural world.

- **Why It Works**: Nature sounds mimic the auditory environment humans evolved in, creating a sense of safety and grounding. They also help mask background noise, making them ideal for meditation or relaxation.

- **How to Use It**: Create a soothing environment by playing nature sounds in the background while you work, meditate, or wind down. You can find high-quality recordings on music streaming platforms or nature sound apps.

3. Singing Bowls

Singing bowls—whether made of metal or crystal—produce rich, resonant tones when struck or circled with a mallet. These sounds are believed to promote relaxation, reduce stress, and even improve concentration.

- **How It Works**: The vibrations of the singing bowl create a sense of harmony and balance, which can help quiet the mind and center your focus. Each tone resonates with specific frequencies thought to correspond to different energy centers (or chakras) in the body.

- **How to Use It**: You can attend a sound bath session in person, where practitioners use multiple bowls to create a meditative soundscape, or try recordings of singing bowls online. If you're feeling adventurous, purchase a bowl and experiment with creating your own calming tones at home.

4. Mantras and Chanting

Mantras and chants are simple, repetitive phrases or sounds that can help focus the mind and promote a sense of peace. Common examples include the Sanskrit mantra "Om" or phrases like "I am calm" or "This too shall pass."

- **Why It Works**: Repetition of a mantra creates a rhythmic focus, allowing the mind to settle and quiet intrusive thoughts. Pairing the mantra with deep breathing amplifies its calming effects.

- **How to Use It**: Find a comfortable seated position, close your eyes, and repeat your chosen mantra aloud or silently. You can pair it with soft background music or chanting tracks for a more immersive experience.

5. Drumming and Rhythm

Drumming has been used in cultural rituals and healing practices for centuries. Its steady rhythm can create a trance-like state, making it a powerful tool for mindfulness and emotional release.

- **Why It Works**: Rhythmic drumming synchronizes with your heartbeat, creating a sense of grounding and connection. It's also a highly engaging practice that demands your full attention, pulling you into the present moment.

- **How to Use It**: If you don't have access to a drum, try hand clapping or tapping a surface in time with a beat. Alternatively, listen to recordings of drumming circles or rhythmic tracks designed for meditation.

Incorporating Sound Therapy into Your Routine

Now that you know the basics, let's explore how to make sound therapy a regular part of your life:

1. Schedule Time for Sound: Carve out 5–10 minutes a day to immerse yourself in sound therapy. It could be part of your morning routine, a mid-afternoon break, or an evening wind-down ritual.

2. Create a Dedicated Space: Find a quiet corner where you can relax without interruptions. Add cozy elements like cushions, candles, or dim lighting to create a calming atmosphere.

3. Combine with Other Practices: Pair sound therapy with mindfulness exercises like deep breathing, yoga, or journaling. For example, listen to binaural beats while meditating or play nature sounds during a gentle yoga session.

4. Experiment with Techniques: Try out different sound therapy methods to discover what resonates with you. Maybe you're drawn to the vibrations of a singing bowl, or perhaps nature sounds feel more grounding. There's no right or wrong—it's all about finding what works for you.

5. Reflect on the Experience: After each session, take a moment to notice how you feel. Are you calmer, more focused, or simply lighter? Write down your observations to track the benefits and deepen your mindfulness practice.

The Power of Sound

Sound therapy is more than just listening—it's a full sensory experience that can transform your mental and emotional state. Whether it's the gentle hum of a singing bowl, the rhythmic beat of a drum, or the soothing sound of rain, each technique offers a unique way to connect with yourself and the present moment.

By incorporating sound therapy into your mindfulness routine, you're giving yourself a powerful tool for relaxation, focus, and self-care. So, pick a technique, press play, and let the sound guide you to a place of peace and balance.

Incorporating Music and Sound into Daily Life

Bringing music and sound therapy into your routine doesn't have to be complicated or time-consuming.

Here's how to start:

1. Set Aside Time: Dedicate five minutes a day to your musical mindfulness practice. It could be during your morning coffee, your lunch break, or just before bed.

2. Create a Cozy Space: Find a comfortable spot where you can unwind. Dim the lights, light a candle, or add a cozy blanket to set the mood.

3. Tune In: Press play on your playlist or sound therapy track. Close your eyes, take a few deep breaths, and let the sounds wash over you.

4. Reflect: After your session, pause for a moment to notice how you feel. Are you more relaxed? Focused? Energized? Jot down any observations in a journal to track your progress.

5. Experiment: There's no one-size-fits-all approach. Try different genres, instruments, and techniques to find what works best for you.

Why It Matters

In today's fast-paced world, finding moments of calm can feel like searching for a needle in a haystack. Our minds are constantly pulled in different directions—work deadlines, personal responsibilities, and the never-ending buzz of notifications. It's no wonder so many of us feel overwhelmed.

This is where music and sound therapy come in. Unlike some mindfulness practices that require significant time or effort, sound offers an accessible, simple way to reset. Whether you're pausing to enjoy a favorite song or immersing yourself in the tones of a singing bowl, sound provides a unique shortcut to mindfulness—a bridge between the chaos of life and the clarity you're seeking.

A Universal Language

One of the most remarkable things about music and sound is their universality. No matter your age, culture, or background, sound has the power to resonate with you. A soothing melody or a calming rhythm can cut through barriers and speak directly to your emotions in a way that words often cannot.

This makes sound a particularly effective mindfulness tool. It doesn't demand intellectual engagement or prior experience—it simply invites you to listen. In that moment, you're not worrying about your to-do list or analyzing your next step; you're just present.

Science Meets Simplicity

The benefits of sound therapy are deeply rooted in science. Research has shown that sound can influence brainwave activity, shifting your mental state from stress and overthinking to calm and focused. Listening to specific types of music or tones activates the parasympathetic nervous system, the part of your body responsible for rest and relaxation.

But what makes this practice truly special is its simplicity. You don't need hours of free time or elaborate equipment. A five-minute playlist or a few moments with nature sounds can have a noticeable impact on your mood and mental clarity. It's mindfulness made practical, designed to fit into even the busiest of days.

A Catalyst for Emotional Connection

Sound doesn't just soothe—it connects. It connects you to yourself, helping you explore and process emotions you might otherwise overlook. It connects you to others, creating shared experiences through song or rhythm. And it connects you to the world around you, reminding you of the beauty in something as simple as a bird's song or a rustling breeze.

In a time when it's easy to feel disconnected—whether from ourselves or the people we care about—sound offers a gentle way to bridge the gap. It helps us slow down, tune in, and appreciate the moments that matter most.

A Tool for Lifelong Mindfulness

Unlike trends that come and go, sound is timeless. It's a tool you can use throughout your life, adapting it to your needs and preferences as you grow. Whether it's a playlist that calms you during a stressful commute or a sound bath that grounds you during challenging times, the versatility of sound makes it an enduring ally in your mindfulness journey.

A Better World Through Mindful Listening

When you prioritize mindful practices like sound therapy, the benefits extend beyond you. A calmer, more centered you can navigate life with greater patience, empathy, and resilience. This ripple effect touches your relationships, your work, and your community.

In a world that often feels noisy and overwhelming, learning to listen—truly listen—can be transformative. By embracing sound as a mindfulness tool, you're not just nurturing your own well-being; you're contributing to a more mindful, harmonious world.

Sound matters because *you* matter. It's not just about tuning out dis tractions—it's about tuning into the rhythms of life, the melody of your emotions, and the harmony within yourself. So, press play, take a deep breath, and let the sounds guide you toward a more present and balanced way of living.

Take the Challenge

Ready to explore the role of music in mindfulness? Here's your challenge:

1. Create a five-minute playlist today and save it somewhere easy to access.

2. Set aside time to listen—just five minutes—to your playlist or sound therapy technique.

3. Reflect on how it feels and experiment with new tracks or sounds throughout the week.

Every time you press play, you're taking a step toward greater mindfulness and balance. So, turn up the volume, close your eyes, and let the music work its magic!

Takeaway

Music is a powerful mindfulness tool that can calm your mind, uplift your spirit, and enhance focus. Whether it's listening to a soothing melody, creating your own rhythms, or incorporating soundscapes into your meditation, music offers endless opportunities to ground yourself in the present moment.

Experiment with how you use music today—play a calming playlist during your commute, listen to nature sounds while working, or let your favorite song guide a mindful breathing practice. Notice how sound transforms your state of mind.

As music helps you tune into your emotions, journaling offers a space to explore and express them. In the next chapter, we'll delve into how putting your thoughts on paper can bring clarity, focus, and self-awareness to your mindfulness journey.

Chapter Fifteen

Journaling for Clarity and Focus

Your mind is a constant swirl of thoughts, ideas, and emotions—some clear and actionable, others tangled and overwhelming. Amid this mental chatter, clarity and focus can feel like rare gems buried beneath the noise. Journaling offers a way to unearth those gems, helping you turn the chaos of your mind into something ordered, insightful, and empowering.

Far more than just putting pen to paper, journaling is a practice rooted in science and steeped in benefits. It provides a private space to reflect, process, and organize your thoughts, acting as both a mirror and a map. With each word you write, you're not just documenting your life—you're decluttering your mind, regulating your emotions, solving problems, and even enhancing your memory and learning.

The Science of Journaling

Journaling's benefits aren't just anecdotal; they're well-documented in research. Studies have shown that expressive writing can reduce stress, boost immune function, and improve mental health. When you journal, you activate the parts of your brain responsible for processing emotions, enhancing self-awareness, and improving decision-making.

In fact, writing down your thoughts triggers the brain's left hemisphere, which governs logic and analysis. At the same time, it frees up your right hemisphere, which handles creativity and intuition. This combination helps you gain clarity and think more holistically about your challenges and goals.

Decluttering the Mind

Have you ever felt overwhelmed by the sheer volume of thoughts competing for your attention? Journaling acts as a mental declutterer, allowing you to offload those swirling ideas onto paper. Once your thoughts are out of your head and in front of you, they become easier to understand and prioritize.

Think of it as tidying a messy desk. Before journaling, everything feels chaotic; afterward, there's space to think, breathe, and focus. This simple act of organizing your thoughts can create a sense of calm, helping you approach your day with greater ease and intention.

Emotional Regulation

Journaling isn't just a tool for clarity—it's a lifeline for emotional balance. When you put your feelings into words, you're processing them in a way that helps you understand and manage them. Whether you're venting about frustrations, exploring your fears, or celebrating your wins, journaling provides a safe space to work through emotions without judgment.

Research shows that writing about difficult experiences can reduce their emotional intensity. By expressing your feelings on the page, you create distance from them, making it easier to approach challenges with calm and perspective. Over time, this practice builds emotional resilience, helping you navigate life's ups and downs with greater ease.

Enhancing Problem-Solving

When faced with a tough decision or a lingering problem, your thoughts can feel like an endless loop of "what ifs." Journaling breaks that loop by helping you organize your thoughts, explore options, and gain new insights.

As you write, patterns emerge. You start to see connections you hadn't noticed before, uncover creative solutions, and clarify your next steps. Whether you're brainstorming a big idea or untangling a conflict, journaling transforms abstract thoughts into actionable plans.

Memory and Learning

Writing things down doesn't just help you stay organized—it solidifies your memory and deepens your learning. When you journal about your day, reflect on lessons learned, or summarize key insights, you're engaging the brain in active recall—a process proven to enhance retention and understanding.

Imagine keeping a journal during a period of personal growth or while working toward a big goal. As you document your progress, you're creating a record of valuable lessons and experiences that you can revisit and build upon. Journaling becomes both a tool for learning in the moment and a resource for reflection and growth over time.

Your Journaling Practice Begins Here

In this chapter, we'll explore how to make journaling a powerful part of your daily routine. Whether you're seeking clarity, emotional release, or creative breakthroughs, you'll discover techniques tailored to your needs. From guided prompts to freewriting exercises, journaling offers endless ways to sharpen your focus, deepen your self-awareness, and unlock the full potential of your mind.

Let's dive into the transformative power of putting pen to paper.

Journaling Techniques to Try

1. The Brain Dump

Purpose: Unload mental clutter and create a sense of calm.

How It Works:

- Set a timer for five minutes.

- Write down everything on your mind, without filtering or organizing.

- Let the thoughts flow freely, from worries to ideas to to-do lists.

This technique is perfect for starting your day with a clear head or winding down at night.

2. Gratitude Journaling

Purpose: Shift your mindset toward positivity and appreciation.

How It Works:

- Write down three things you're grateful for today.

- Be specific: instead of "I'm grateful for my family," try "I'm grateful for the laugh I shared with my daughter at breakfast."

Gratitude journaling has been shown to boost mood, improve relation
ships, and increase overall happiness.

3. Guided Prompts

Purpose: Spark reflection and insight with structured questions.

How It Works: Choose one of these prompts to explore:

- What's weighing on my mind today, and why?

- What's one thing I want to let go of?

- What are three things I'd like to accomplish this week?

Prompts are ideal for beginners or anyone seeking direction in their
writing.

4. Daily Intentions Journaling

Purpose: Start your day with focus and clarity.

How It Works:

- Write a short statement about how you want to approach the
  day.

- Example: "Today, I will prioritize progress over perfection."

Setting intentions grounds your day in mindfulness and purpose.

5. Visualization Journaling

Purpose: Clarify goals and build optimism through mental imagery.

How It Works:

- Imagine a specific goal or scenario, like delivering a great presentation or achieving a personal milestone.

- Write about it in detail as though it's already happened.

Visualization boosts confidence and motivates action by reinforcing positive mental imagery.

6. Visual Journaling

Purpose: Tap into creativity and express thoughts without words.

How It Works:

- Instead of writing, sketch, doodle, or create a mind map of your thoughts and feelings.

- Use symbols, colors, or images to represent your ideas.

This technique is perfect for visual learners or when words feel limiting.

Journaling in Real Life: A Case Study

After losing her job, Leah felt stuck in a spiral of self-doubt and anxiety. A friend suggested she try journaling to process her emotions and regain focus. At first, Leah resisted. "I'm not a writer," she said. But eventually, she decided to give it a try.

She started with a simple brain dump every morning, writing down everything that was on her mind. Over time, Leah noticed patterns in her thoughts—fears she needed to confront and strengths she'd overlooked.

One day, she wrote about her ideal career and realized she'd always wanted to start her own business. That spark of insight grew into an actionable plan, and within a year, Leah had launched her own online store.

Journaling didn't just help Leah clear her mind—it became a tool for self-discovery and empowerment.

Practical Applications: Making Journaling Work for You

1. Adapt to Your Schedule

Busy day? Try micro-journaling—just two or three sentences to capture your thoughts.

2. Use Digital Tools

Prefer typing? Apps like Day One or Evernote let you journal on the go.

3. Create a Ritual

Pair journaling with another habit, like your morning coffee or evening wind-down.

4. Keep It Visible

Leave your journal in a place where you'll see it daily, like your bedside table or desk.

Reflect and Apply

1. **Reflect:** What part of your life feels most cluttered or unclear right now? How could journaling help?

2. **Apply:** Choose one journaling technique and try it today. How does it make you feel?

3. **Plan:** Set aside five minutes for journaling daily over the next week.

Takeaway

Journaling is more than just writing—it's a powerful tool for decluttering your mind, processing emotions, and gaining clarity. By dedicating just a few minutes each day to putting your thoughts on paper, you can uncover insights, set intentions, and build a stronger connection with yourself.

Try this: Choose one journaling technique from this chapter, such as guided prompts or free writing. Commit to practicing it daily for a week and reflect on how it impacts your mindset and focus.

With journaling as part of your mindfulness journey, the next step is to bring all the tools you've learned into a cohesive system. In the final chapter, we'll explore how to build a personalized mindfulness toolkit that empowers you to reset and recharge anytime, anywhere.

Chapter Sixteen

Building Your Mindfulness Toolkit

Mindfulness isn't a one-size-fits-all solution; it's a personal journey, shaped by the tools and practices that resonate most with you. Think of mindfulness as a skill set—one that you can refine and expand over time. Just as a carpenter wouldn't rely on a single tool for every project, cultivating mindfulness requires a variety of approaches, each suited to different moments and needs in your life.

Your mindfulness toolkit is your personalized collection of practices de-signed to help you stay present, grounded, and balanced, no matter what life throws your way. Some tools might calm your mind during moments of stress, like breathing exercises or grounding techniques. Others might bring clarity, like journaling or visualization. And then there are the tools that nurture long-term growth, such as gratitude practices or mindful observation. Together, these tools empower you to navigate challenges, find joy in the ordinary, and connect more deeply with yourself and the world around you.

This chapter isn't about prescribing a rigid routine or overwhelming you with techniques—it's about helping you discover what works for you.

Whether you're just starting out or looking to deepen an existing practice, you'll find practical, adaptable tools to suit your unique needs.

Mindfulness isn't about perfection; it's about presence. With your toolkit in hand, you'll have the resources to meet each moment with intention, curiosity, and calm. Let's start building.

How to Build Your Toolkit

1. Identify Your Go-To Tools

Start by reflecting on the techniques that resonated with you the most. Did grounding exercises help you feel more centered? Did gratitude journaling shift your mindset? Choose 2–3 practices to anchor your routine.

2. Create a Routine That Fits Your Life

Mindfulness isn't one-size-fits-all. Whether you have five minutes in the morning or a quiet moment before bed, tailor your toolkit to your schedule.

- **Morning**: Use affirmations or a breathing exercise to start the day with intention.

- **Midday**: Take a movement break or try a grounding technique to reset during a busy afternoon.

- **Evening**: Reflect with gratitude journaling or visualization to wind down.

3. Be Flexible and Adaptable

Life changes, and so will your needs. Your toolkit should evolve with you. If a practice stops resonating, try a new one. If time feels tight, scale back to one-minute resets. The key is to keep showing up, no matter what.

Troubleshooting Common Challenges

Even with the best intentions, building a mindfulness practice can feel challenging at times.

Here's how to overcome common obstacles:

"I don't have time."

- Mindfulness doesn't require hours of effort. Choose a one-minute reset like deep breathing or affirmations.

- Integrate mindfulness into existing routines: practice grounding while waiting in line or visualization during your commute.

"I keep forgetting."

- Set reminders on your phone or place sticky notes in visible areas to cue your practice.

- Pair mindfulness with daily habits, like brushing your teeth or making coffee.

"I'm not feeling the benefits."

- Consistency is key. Give each practice at least a week before deciding if it's right for you.

- Reflect on subtle shifts: Are you feeling slightly calmer, more focused, or less reactive?

Reflective Journal Prompts for Your Toolkit

Use these prompts to evaluate and refine your toolkit over time:

1. Which mindfulness practices have made the biggest difference in my daily life?

2. How do I feel before and after using a particular tool?

3. Are there situations where certain tools work better than others?

4. What new practices would I like to explore?

5. How can I adjust my routine to make mindfulness more consistent?

A Mindful Moment: Ravi's Story

Ravi had always struggled with stress. As a busy parent juggling a demanding job, he often felt like there was no time for himself. When he first learned about mindfulness, it seemed overwhelming—how could he fit one more thing into his day?

Ravi started small. He used the 5-4-3-2-1 grounding technique during moments of stress and repeated affirmations while driving to work. Over time, he added gratitude journaling at night, using it as a way to reflect on the positives in his day.

A year later, Ravi's toolkit has become second nature. He no longer feels like mindfulness is "one more thing" but instead sees it as the foundation that helps him navigate life with more patience and balance.

Your Journey Forward

As you continue to explore mindfulness, remember that it's not about perfection—it's about presence. Some days, you'll find it easier to reset than others. That's okay. Mindfulness is a practice, and every small effort contributes to your growth.

Your toolkit is your companion on this journey.

Use it to:

- Navigate stress with greater ease.

- Cultivate clarity in moments of uncertainty.

- Connect more deeply with yourself and others.

Whether it's a one-minute breathing exercise or a weekly journaling session, every mindful moment matters. Over time, these small resets create profound, lasting change.

Final Reflection

As you close this book, take a moment to acknowledge the journey you've embarked upon. By exploring these simple yet powerful practices, you've equipped yourself with tools to reset, refocus, and find balance—tools that fit into your life exactly as it is.

Throughout these pages, you've seen how even the smallest actions can create meaningful shifts. A single breath can anchor you in the present moment. A mindful observation can reveal beauty in the ordinary. A brief journal entry can unlock clarity and focus. Each of these practices is a reminder that change doesn't require massive effort—just consistent, intentional steps.

But this isn't the end of the road—it's just the beginning. Mindfulness isn't a destination you reach; it's a lifelong practice that grows with you. Some days will feel effortless, and others will challenge your patience and resolve. Both are valuable, and both are part of the process.

As you move forward, keep these truths in mind:

- **You already have what you need.** The tools in this book are designed to work with your life, not against it. Whether it's five minutes in the morning or a mindful pause in the middle of a hectic day, you have the power to reset at any time.

- **Progress, not perfection.** There's no right way to practice mindfulness, only the way that works for you. Trust yourself to adapt these tools to your needs, knowing that each small step contributes to your growth.

- **The ripple effect is real.** By cultivating clarity, focus, and calm within yourself, you create a ripple that impacts your relationships, your work, and the world around you.

Pause for a moment and consider this: What is one practice you've learned that resonates most deeply with you? How might you carry it into your day tomorrow?

This is your mindfulness toolkit—yours to build, refine, and personalize as you grow. Whether you use it to calm a busy mind, navigate challenges, or simply find more joy in the everyday, know that each mindful moment is an investment in your well-being.

The journey continues, one breath, one choice, one mindful moment at a time.

Chapter Seventeen

Summary Guide: Integrating Your 5-Minute Reset Toolkit

This guide offers a practical roadmap for incorporating the tools and techniques from each chapter into your daily or weekly routine. Use it as inspiration to create a personalized schedule that fits your life.

Daily Mindfulness Routine

Morning: Set the Tone

1. **Affirmations for Confidence and Clarity**

- Spend one minute stating affirmations aloud or writing them in your journal.

- Example: "I am calm, capable, and ready to take on the day."

1. **Breathing Exercise for Focus**

- Practice a 2-minute breathing technique, like deep belly breaths or the 4-7-8 method, to center yourself.

Midday: Reset and Recharge

1. **Grounding Techniques for Busy Minds**

- During a break, try the 5-4-3-2-1 technique to anchor yourself in the present.

- Focus on five things you can see, four you can touch, three you can hear, two you can smell, and one you can taste.

1. **Movement Breaks for Mental Clarity**

- Take a 5-minute walk or do gentle stretches at your desk to refresh your mind and body.

Evening: Reflect and Unwind

1. **Journaling for Clarity and Focus**

- Spend 5 minutes writing about your day, using prompts like:

- "What went well today?"

- "What challenges did I face, and how did I handle them?"

1. **Visualization for Calm**

- Before bed, visualize a peaceful scene or reflect on a positive moment from your day. This helps quiet the mind and prepare for restful sleep.

Weekly Mindfulness Practice

Sunday: Plan and Prepare

- Dedicate 10–15 minutes to review your mindfulness practices and adjust your routine as needed.

- Set intentions for the week using affirmations or journaling.

Midweek Reset

- Choose one extended practice, like forest bathing or a mindful nature walk, to refresh your energy and refocus your mindset.

Integrating Practices into Busy Schedules

For days when time feels tight, try these quick resets:

- **1-Minute Affirmations**: Repeat affirmations while brushing your teeth or commuting.

- **Micro-Journaling**: Jot down a single sentence about your mood or goal for the day.

- **Mindful Walking**: Practice awareness during a short walk—notice your steps, breathing, and surroundings.

Customizing Your Routine

Use this guide as a starting point, but feel free to adapt it to your preferences and lifestyle. Your mindfulness toolkit is meant to be flexible—designed to support you in all seasons of life.

Made in the USA
Las Vegas, NV
03 December 2024

13257335R00075